COLORING BOOK
for Toddlers

Animals, Numbers & Shapes to color

AGES 3-5

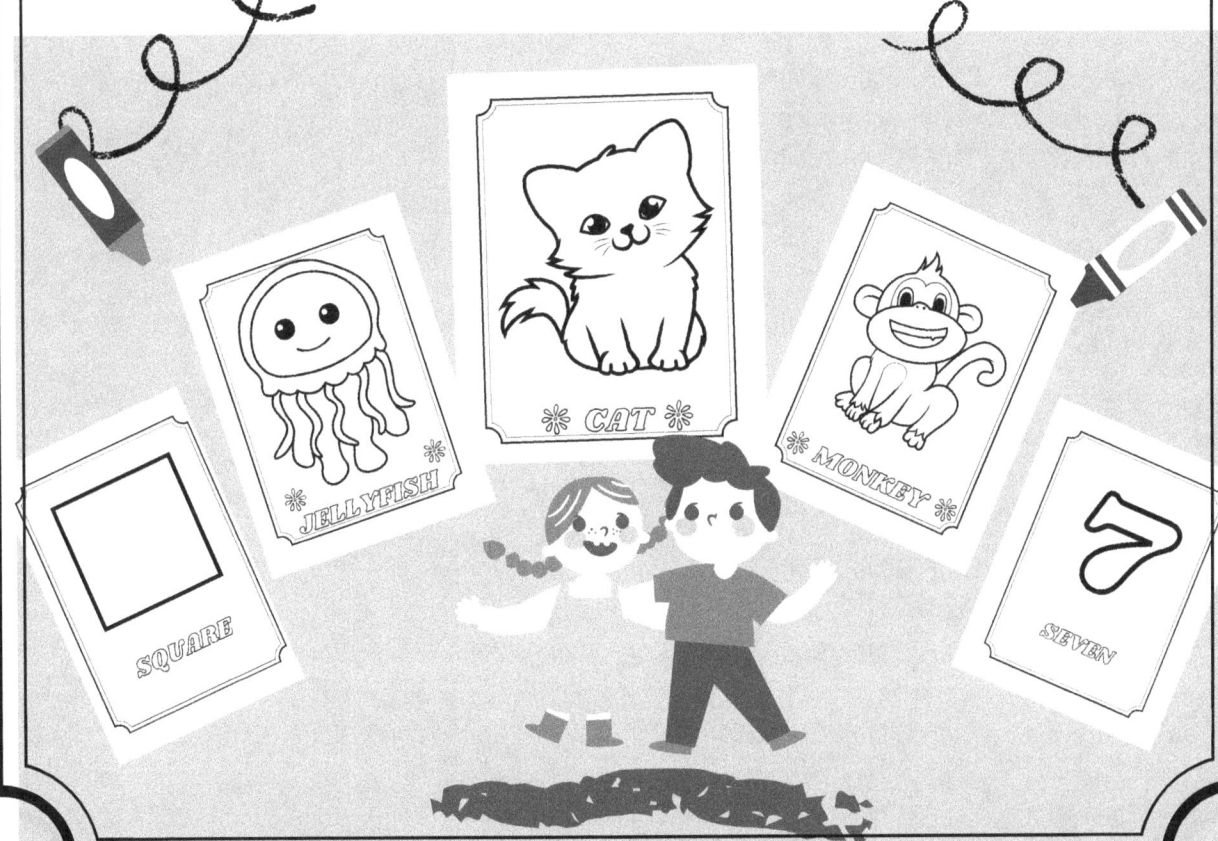

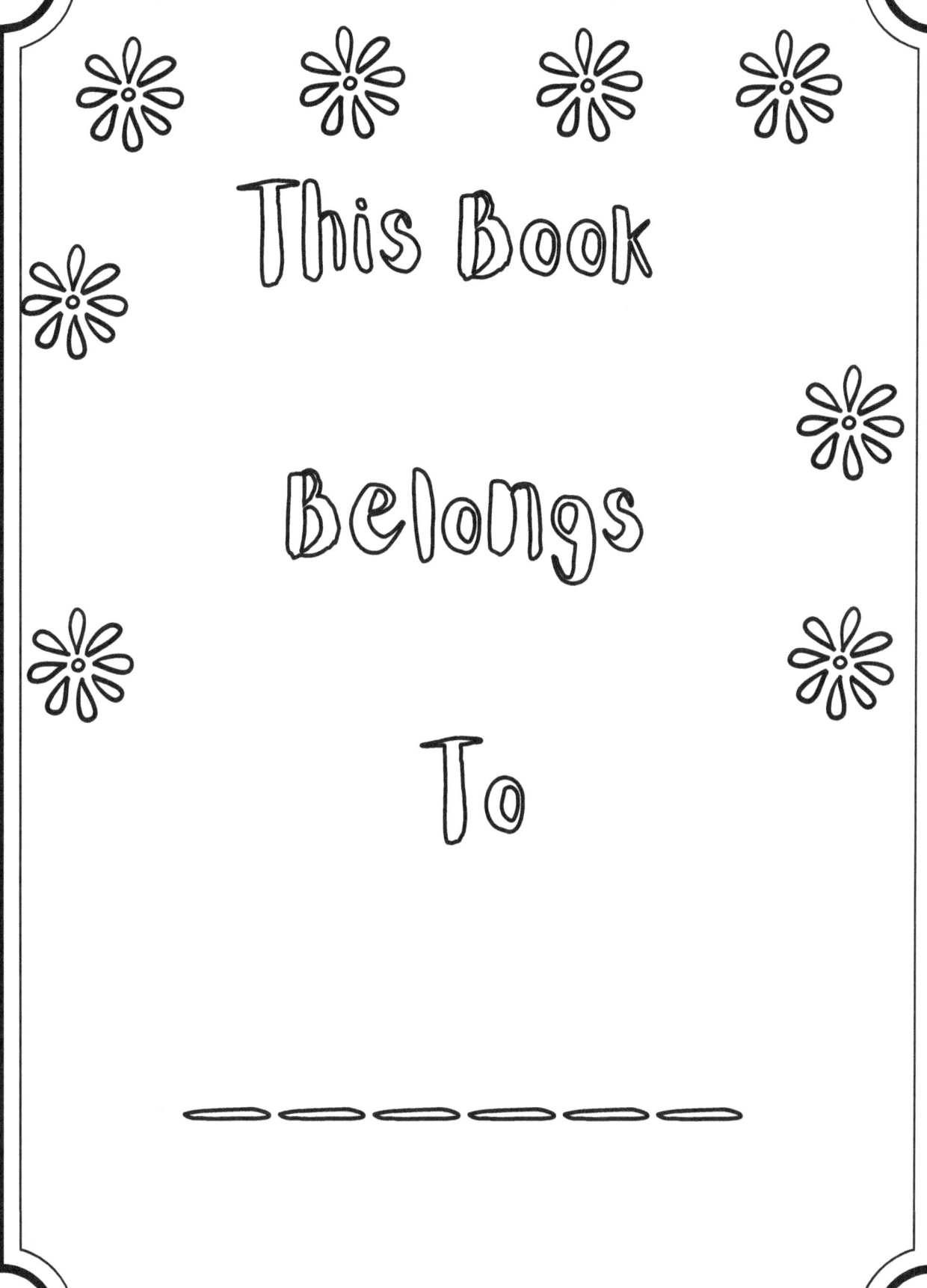

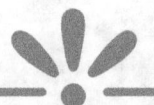

Dear Customer,
Many Thanks for purchasing this Book.
We hope you love it!

As a micro publishing business, we thank you from the bottom
of our hearts for selecting our Book.
Yayyy!

If you enjoy this purchase and would like to support our teeny, tiny
business, please take a moment to leave us a review for it on this book's
Amazon product page. It would help us immensely.

Thank you so much for your Support.
Sincerely,
Troglodyte Publications

Copyright Troglodyte Publications. All rights reserved.
No portion of this book may be reproduced
or used in any way without express permission of the Publisher.

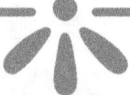

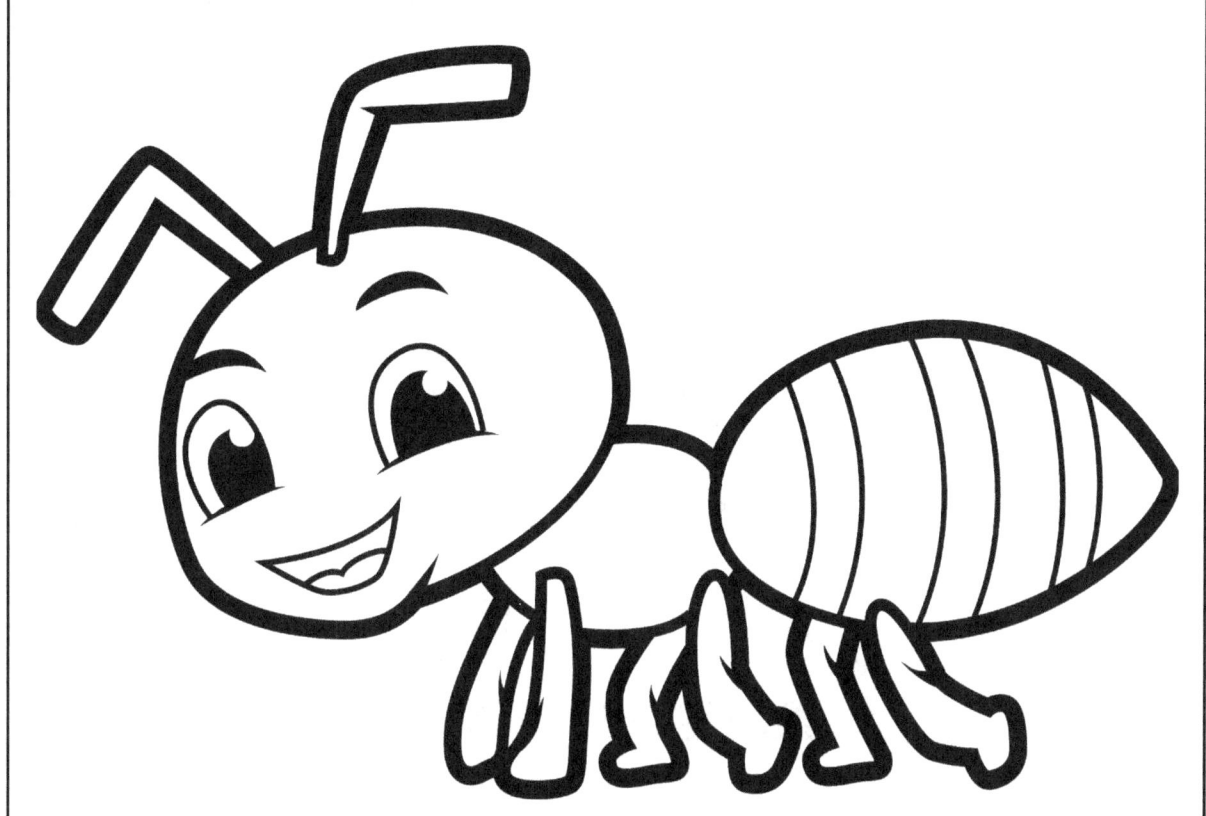

 ANT

1

ONE

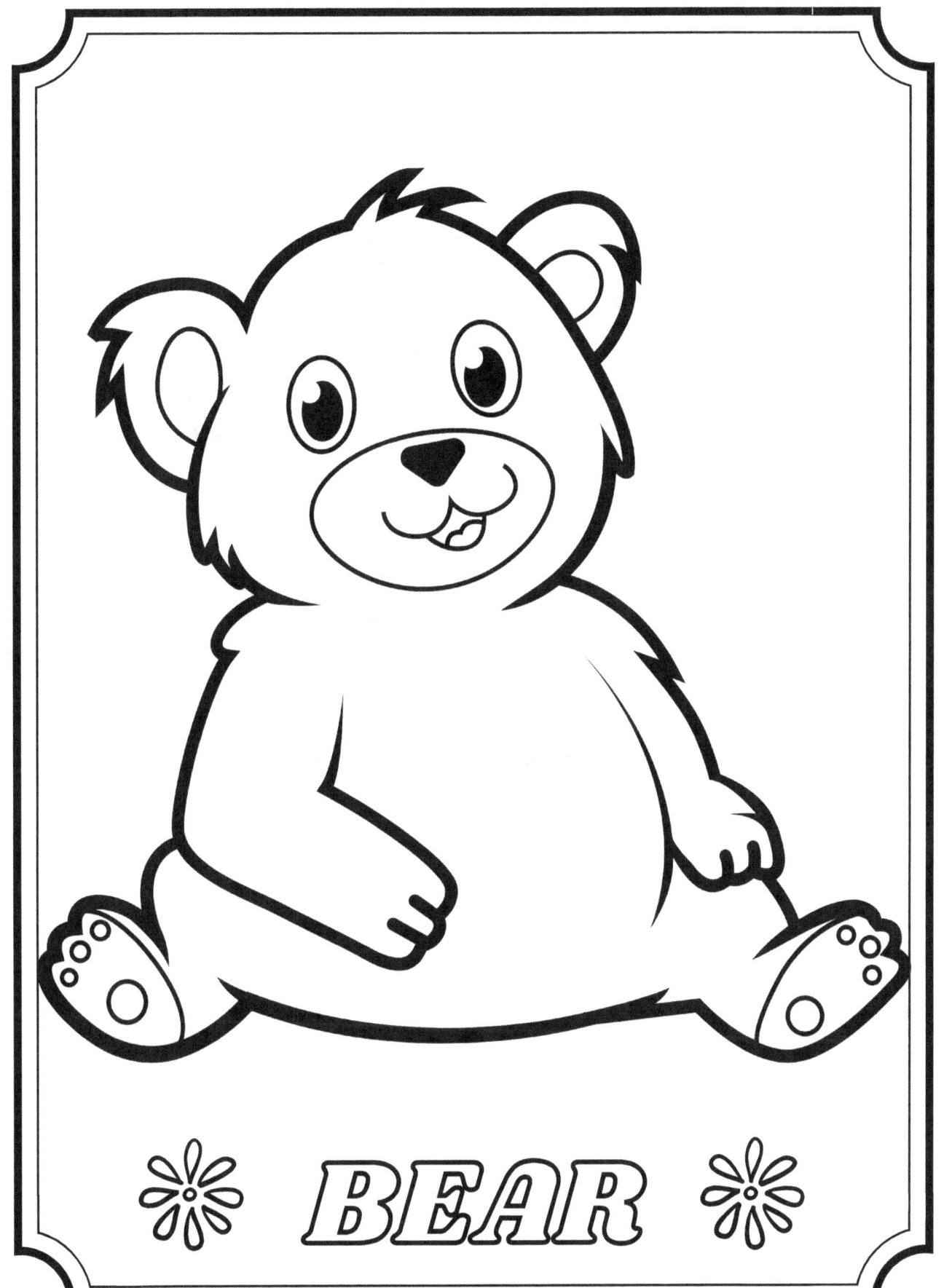

2

TWO

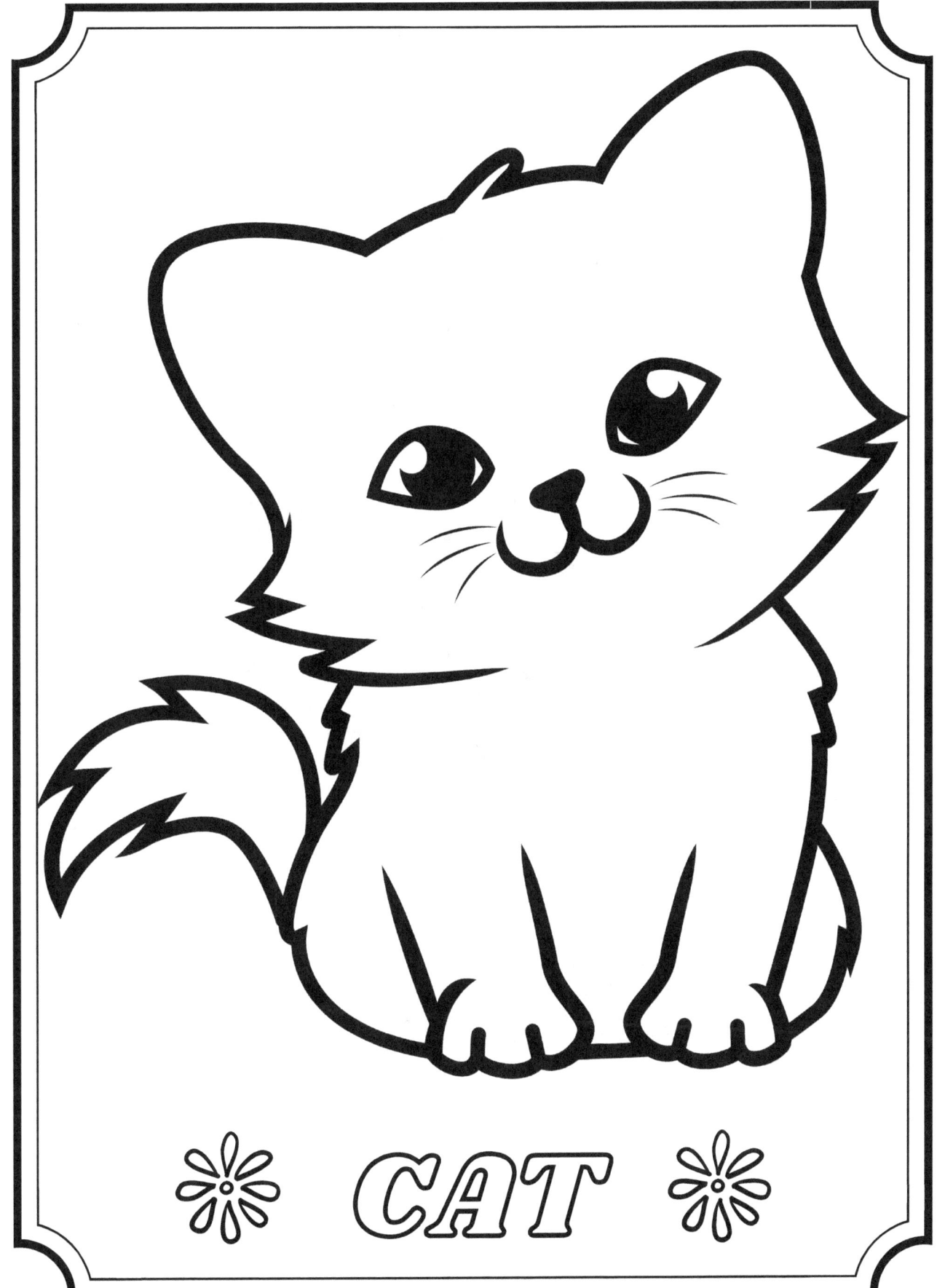

3

THREE

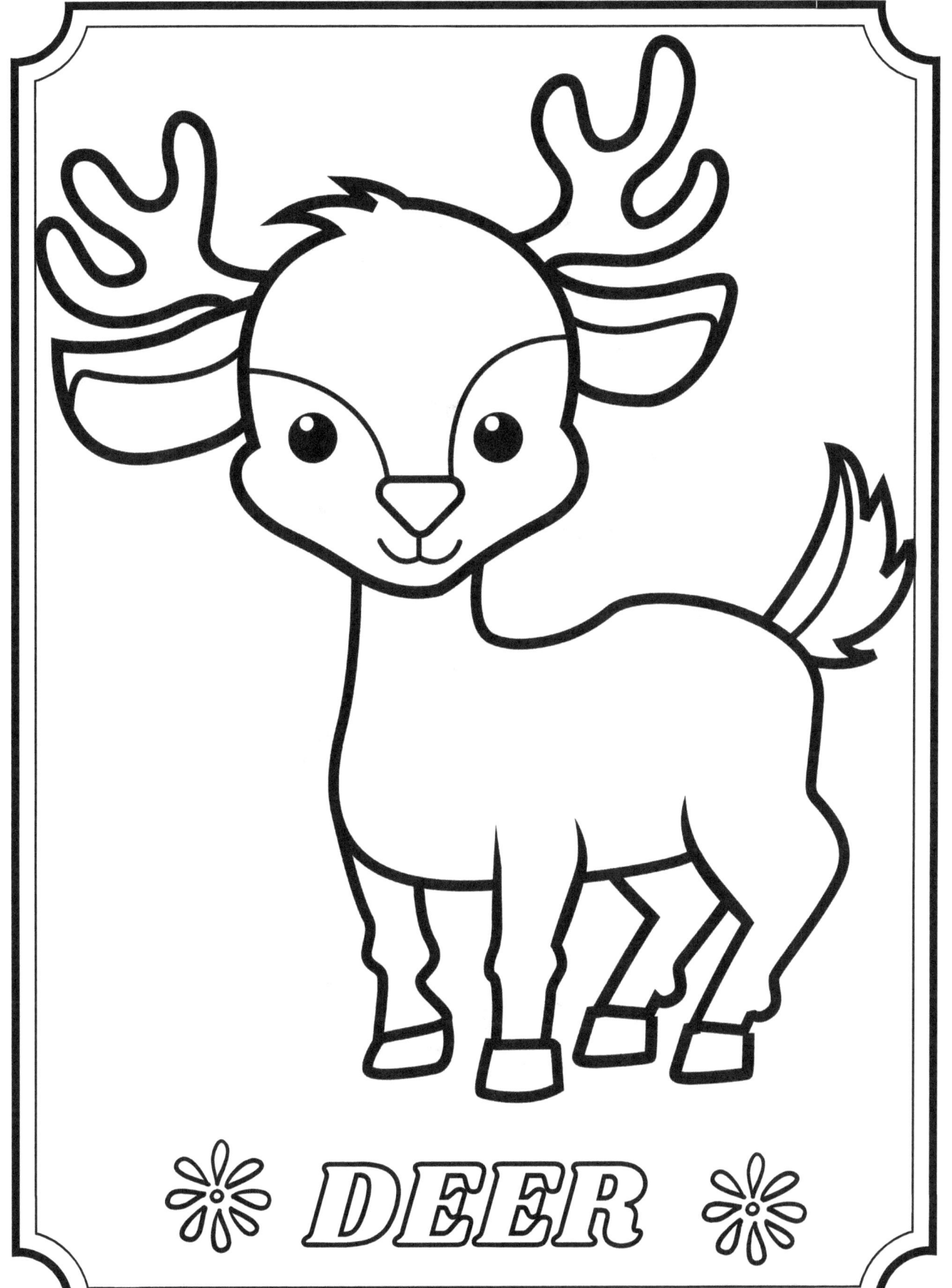

4

FOUR

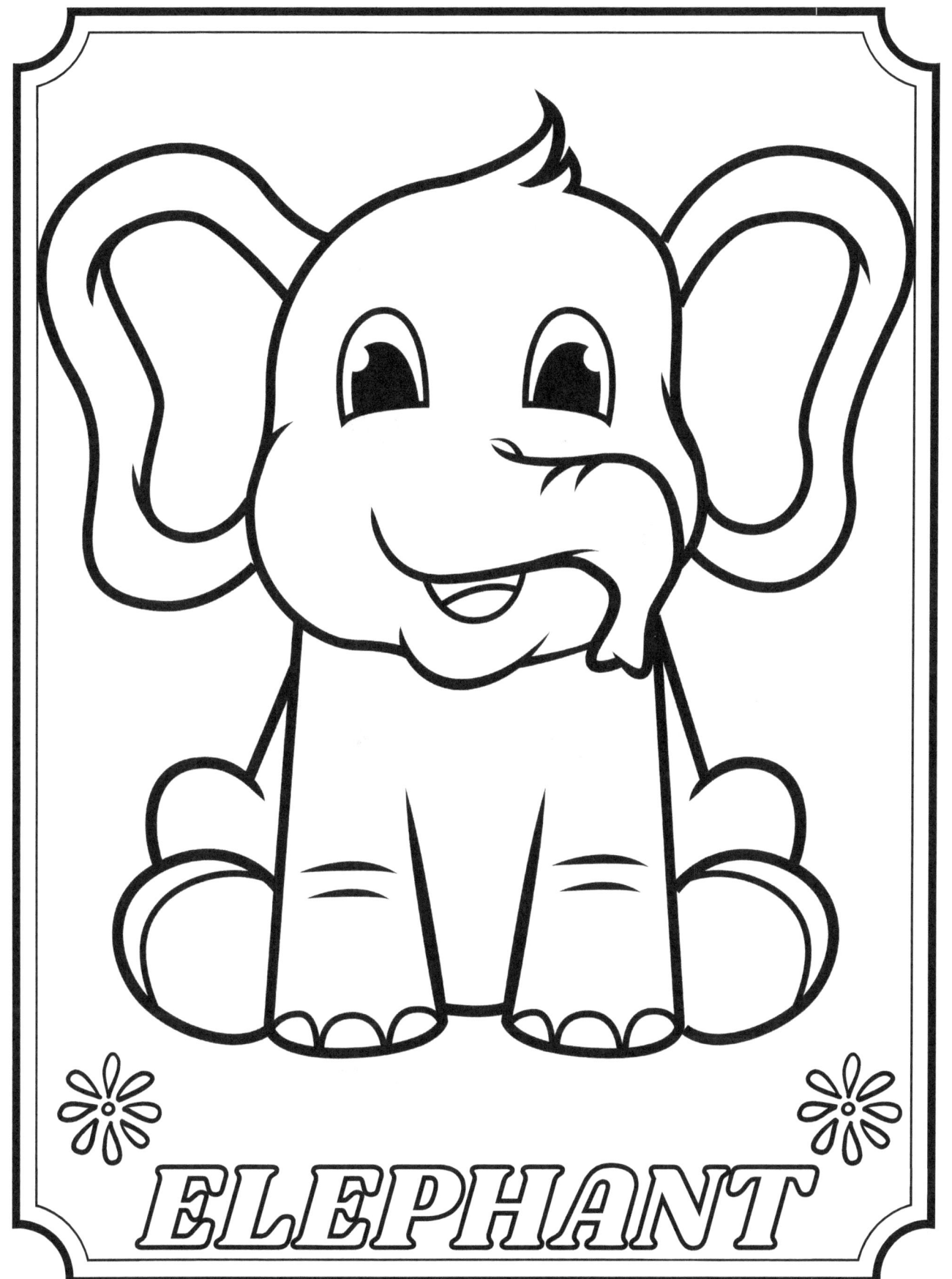

5

FIVE

❊ **FISH** ❊

6

SIX

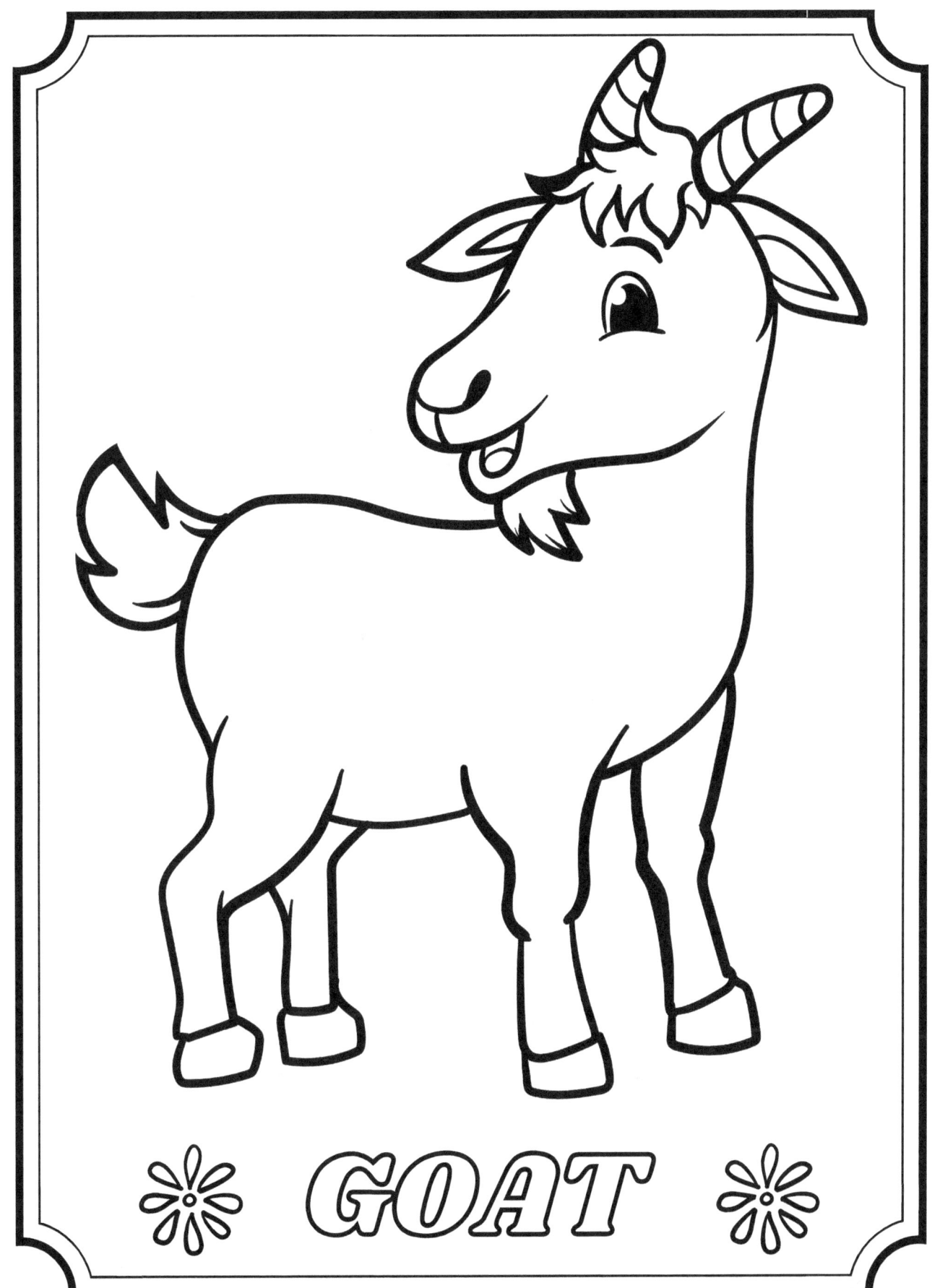

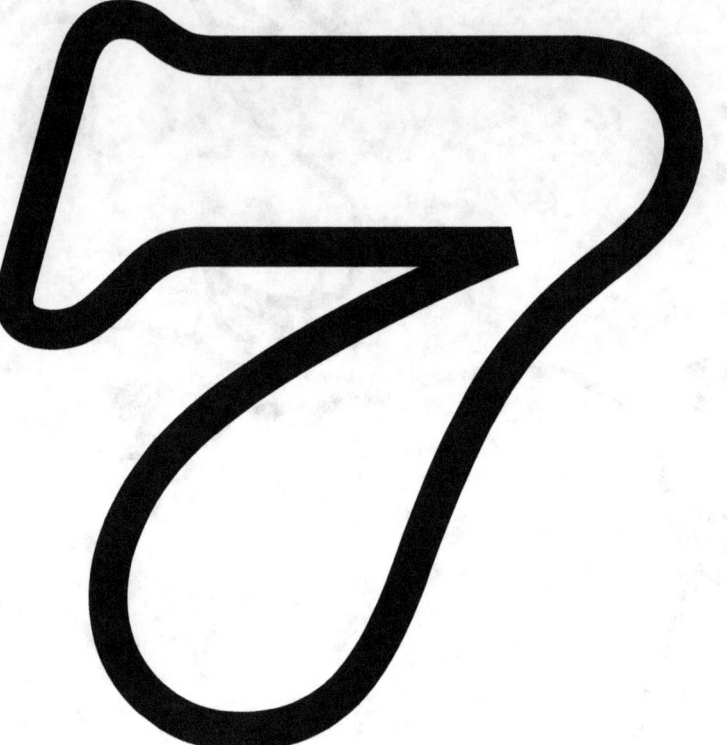

SEVEN

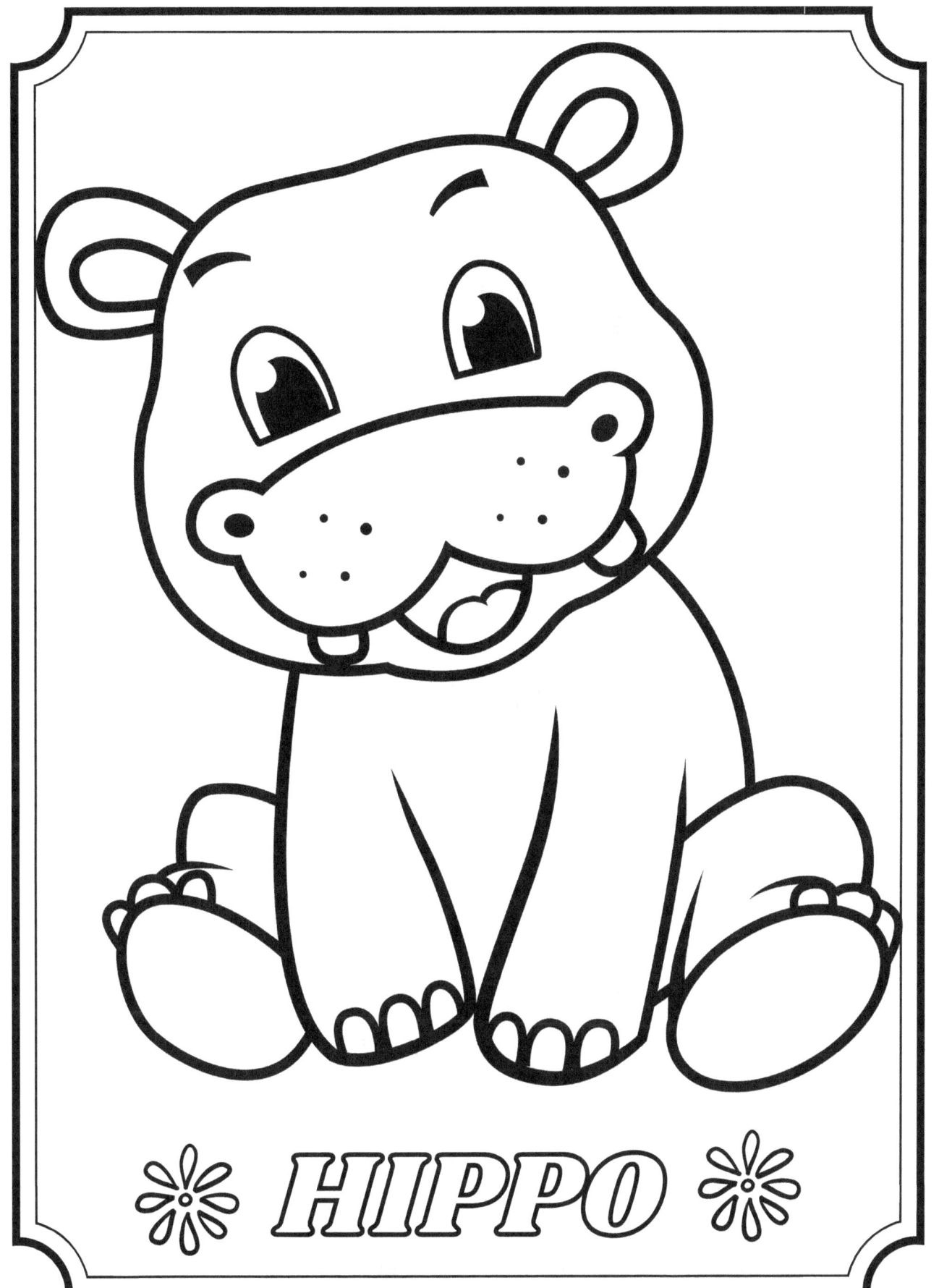

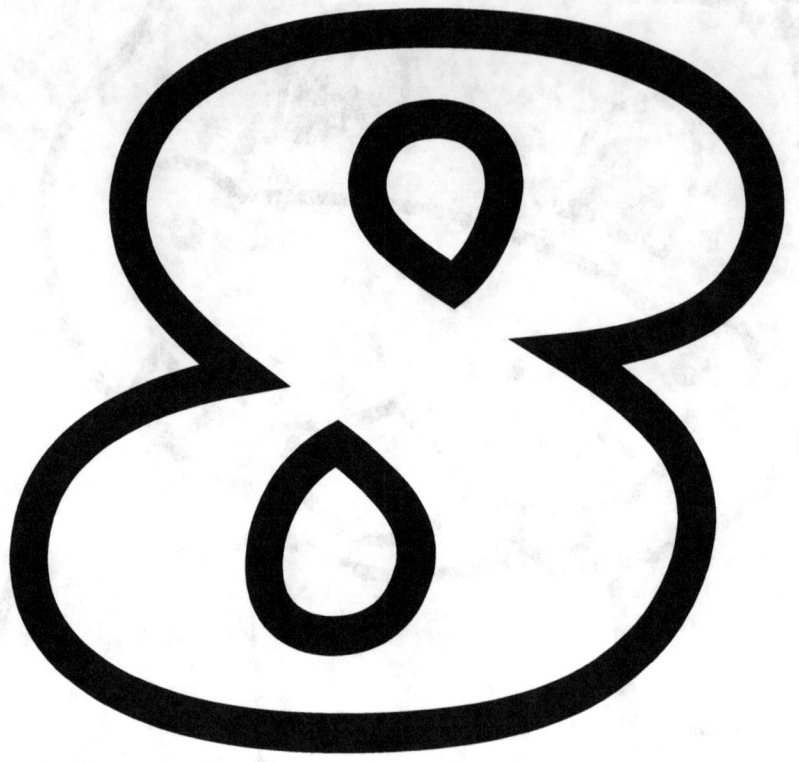

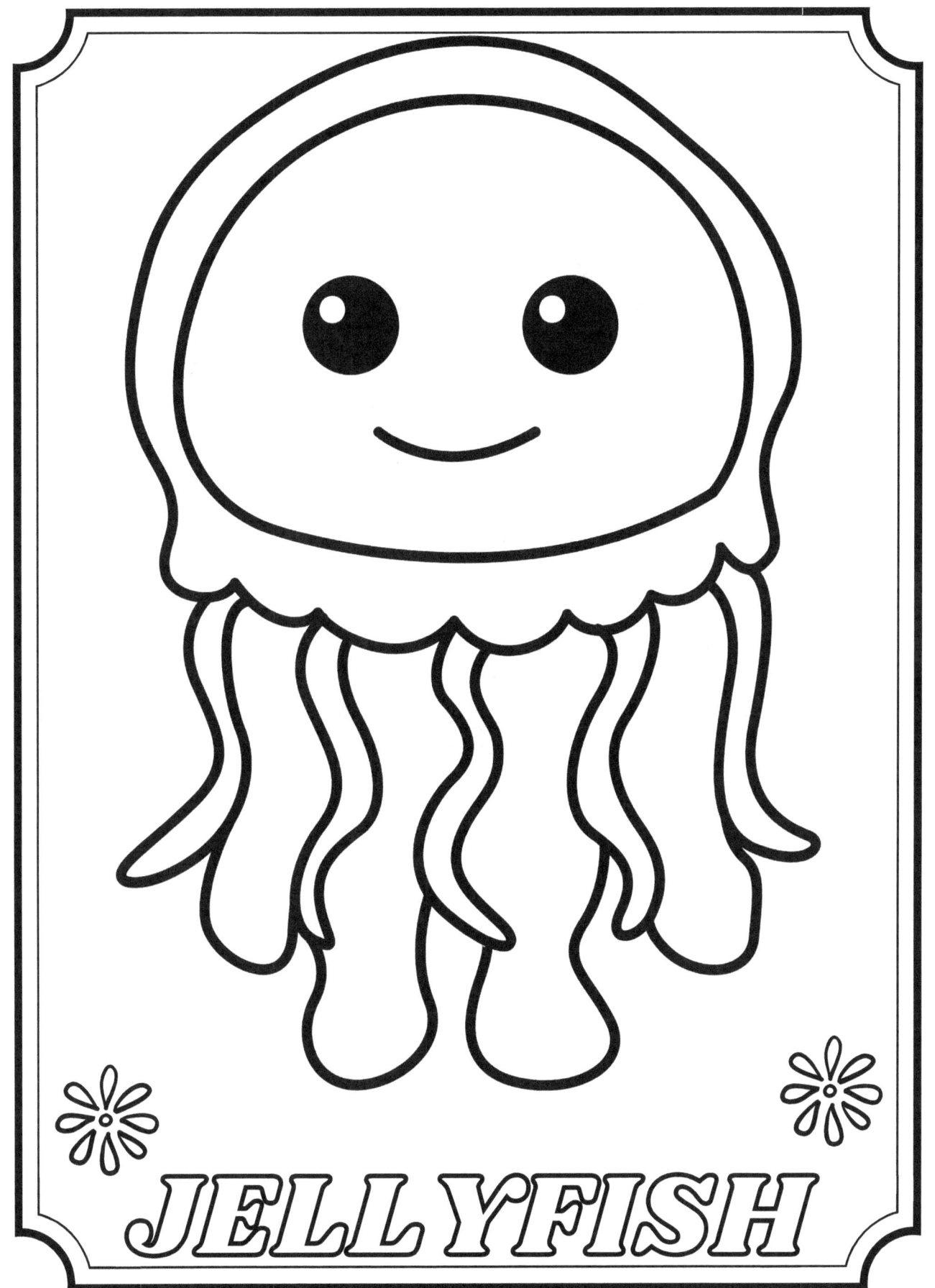

JELLYFISH

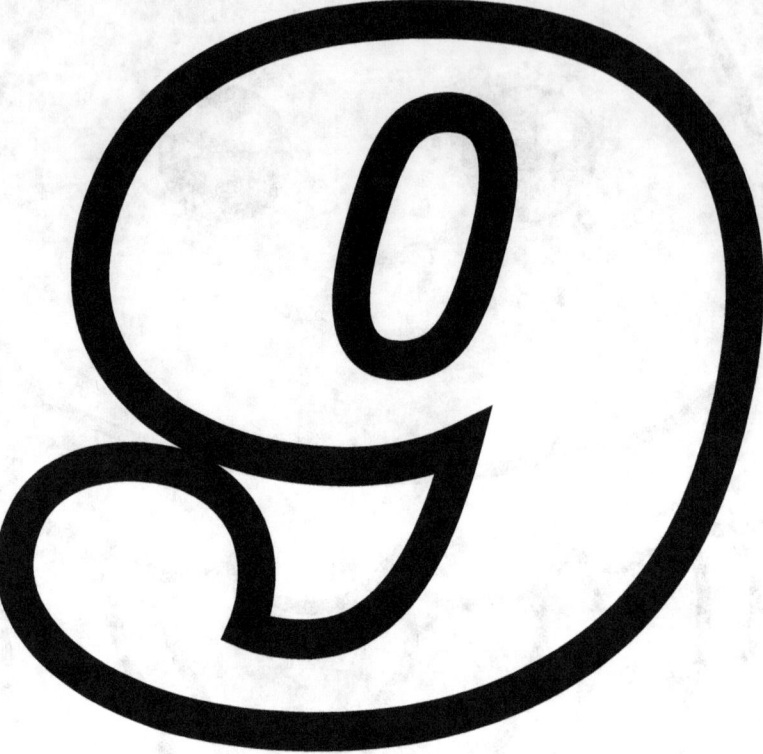

NINE

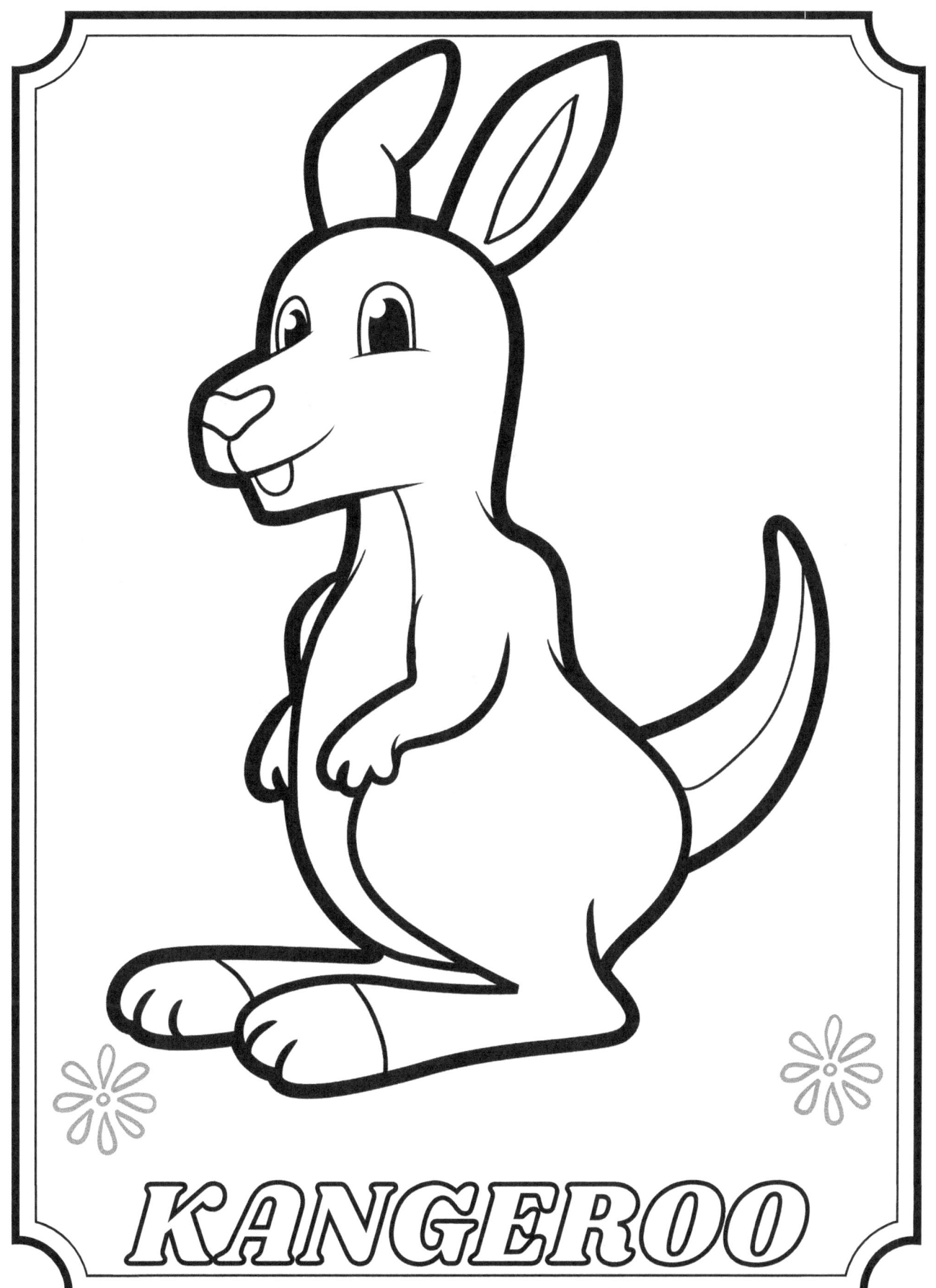

10

TEN

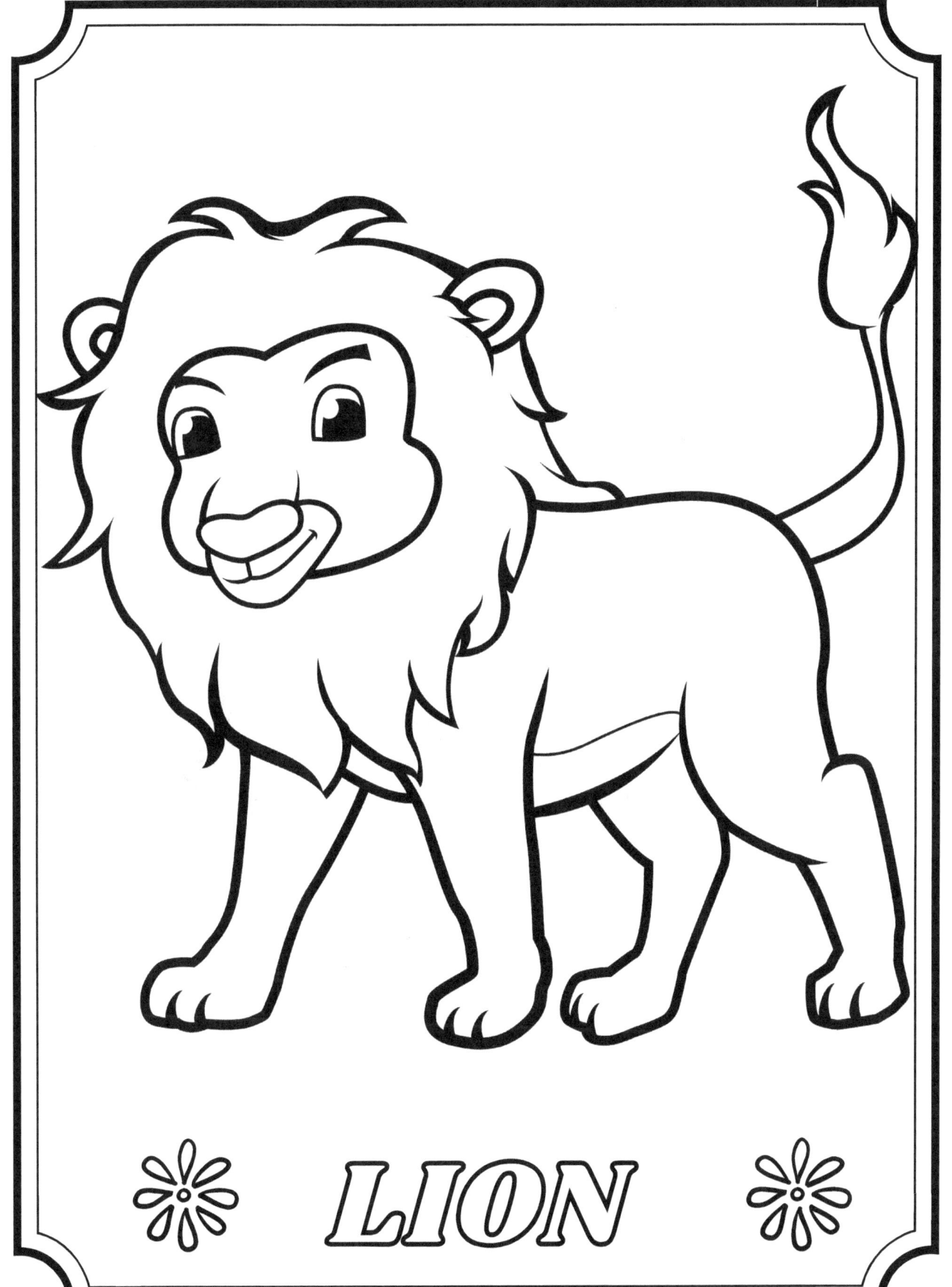

11
ELEVEN

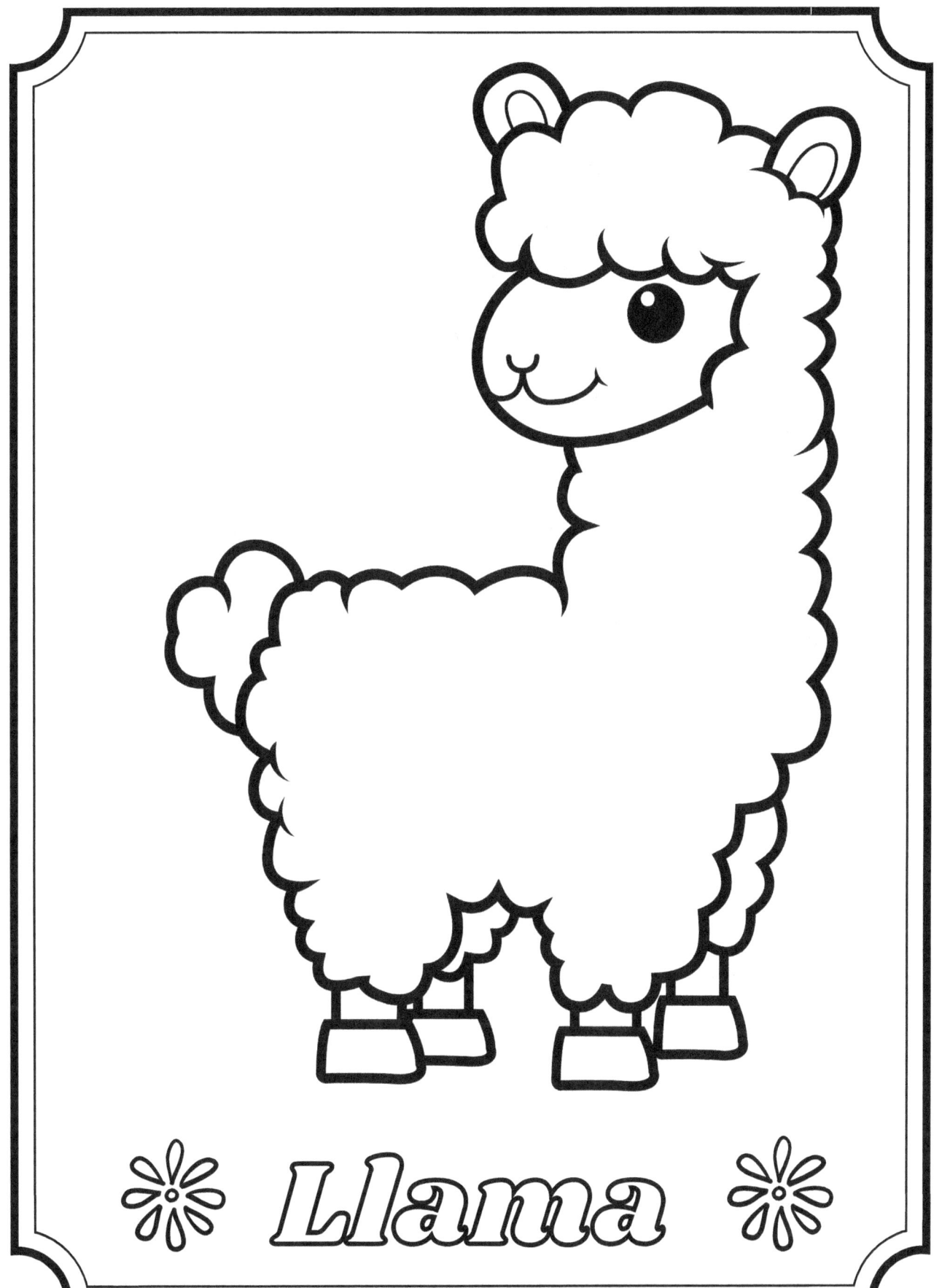

12
TWELVE

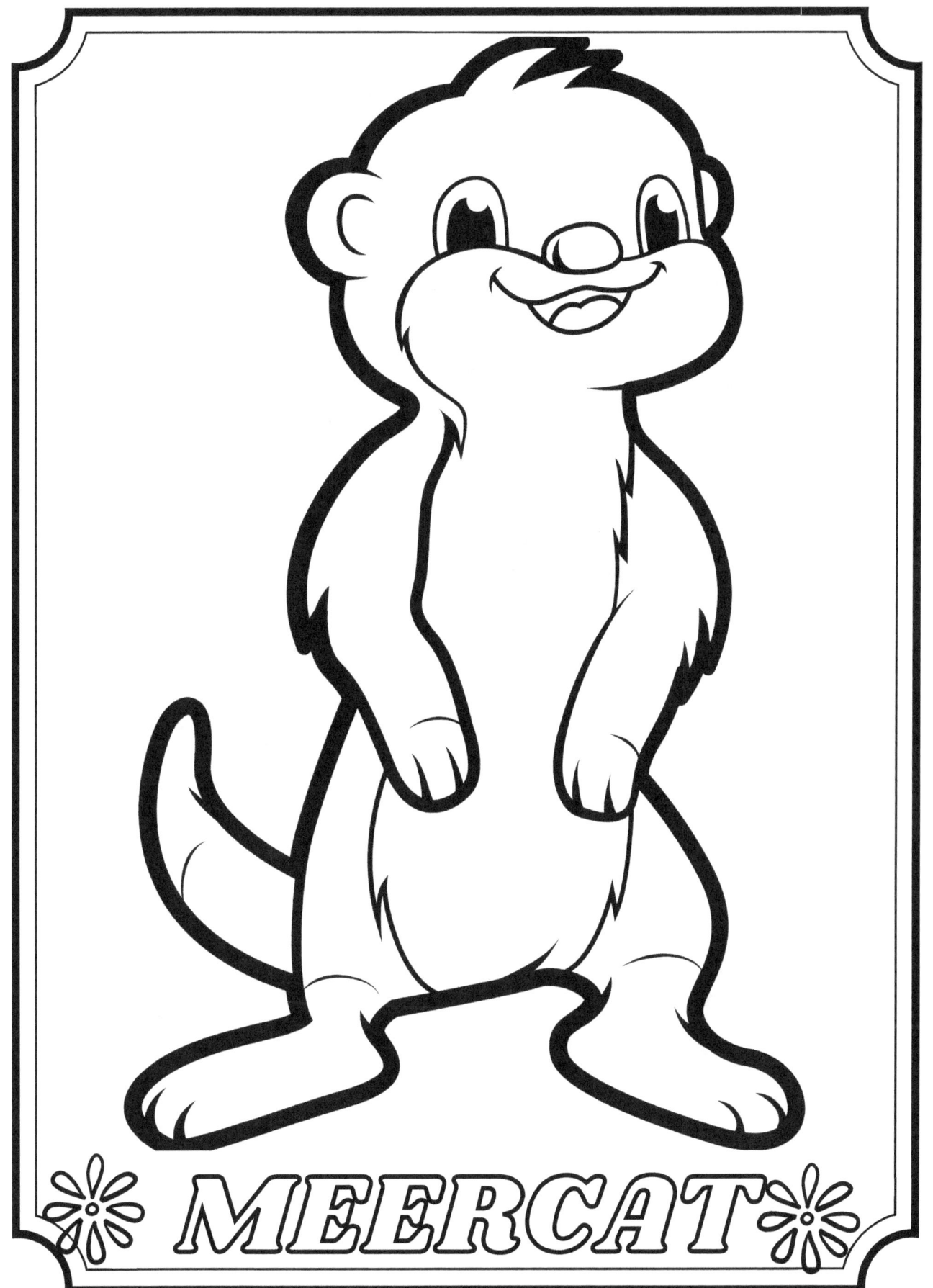

13

THIRTEEN

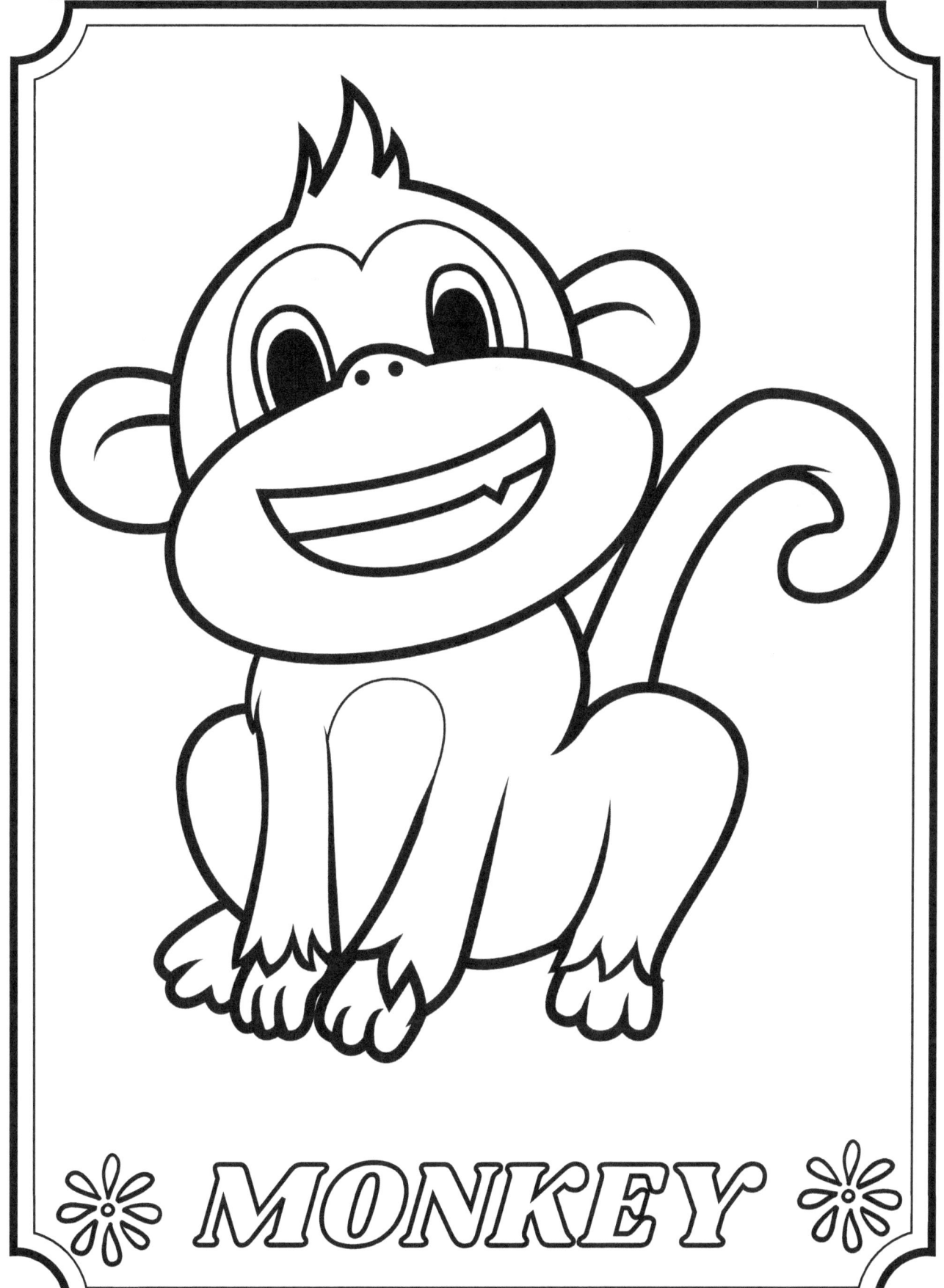

14

FOURTEEN

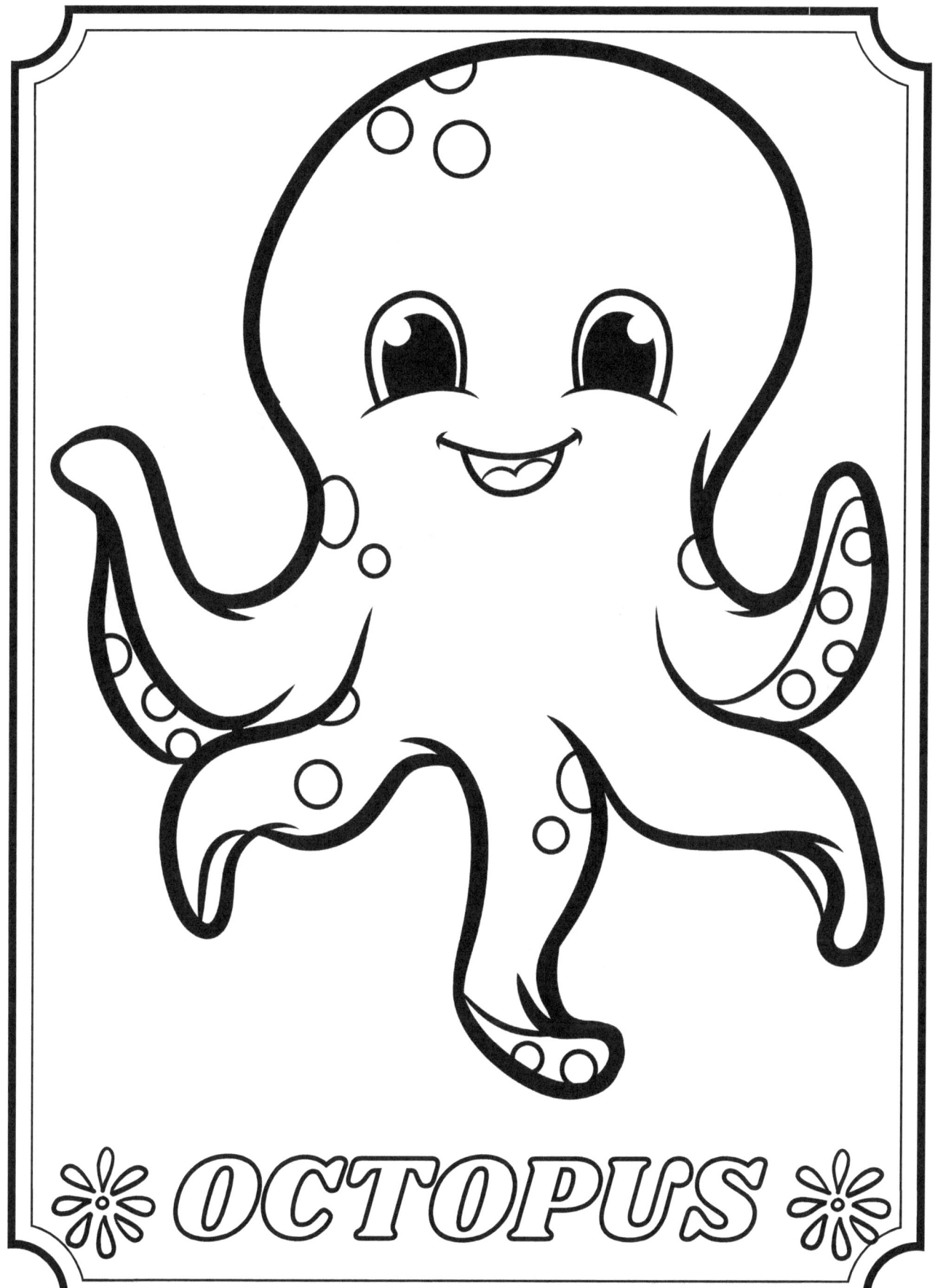

15

FIFETEEN

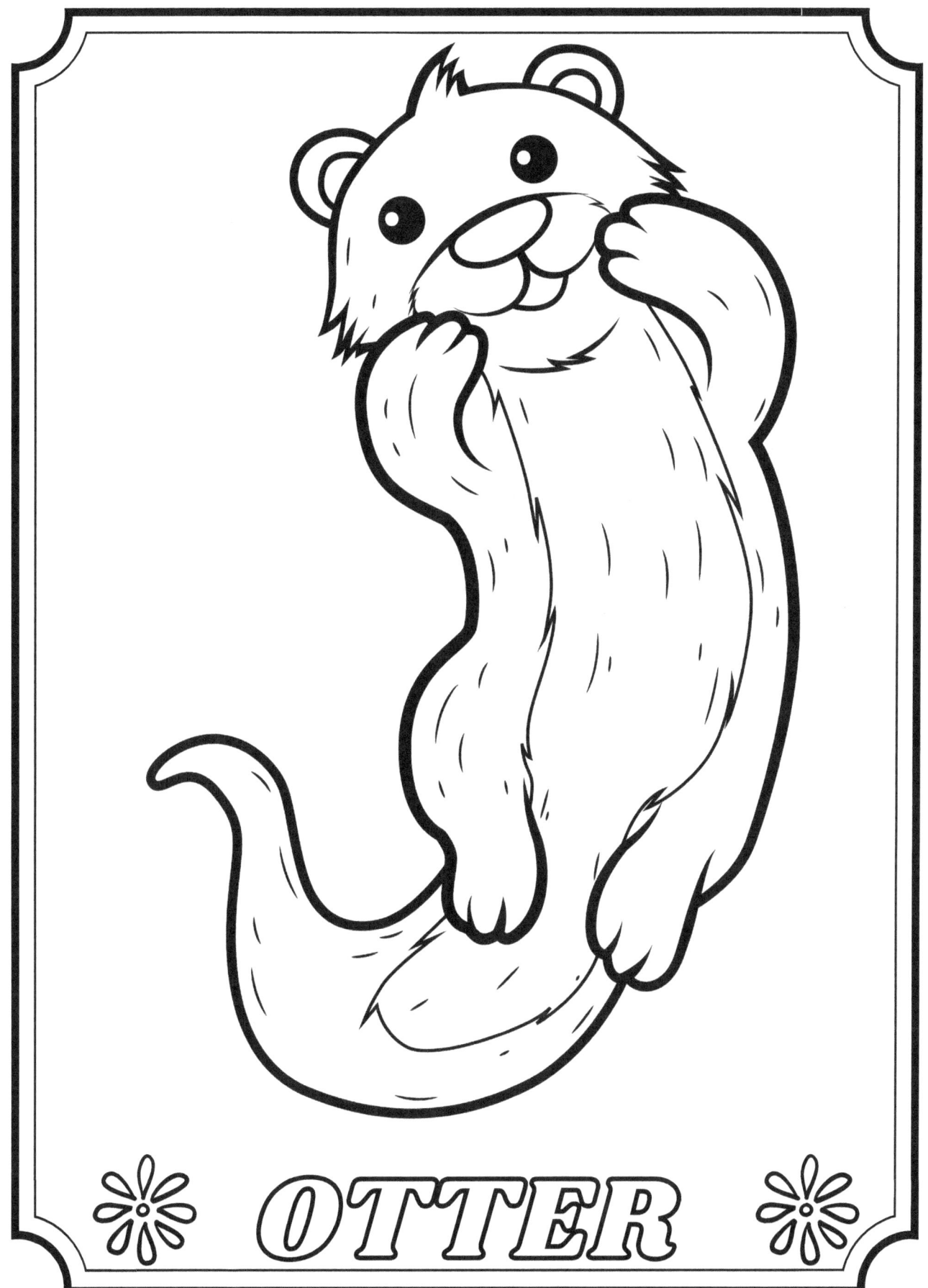

16

SIXTEEN

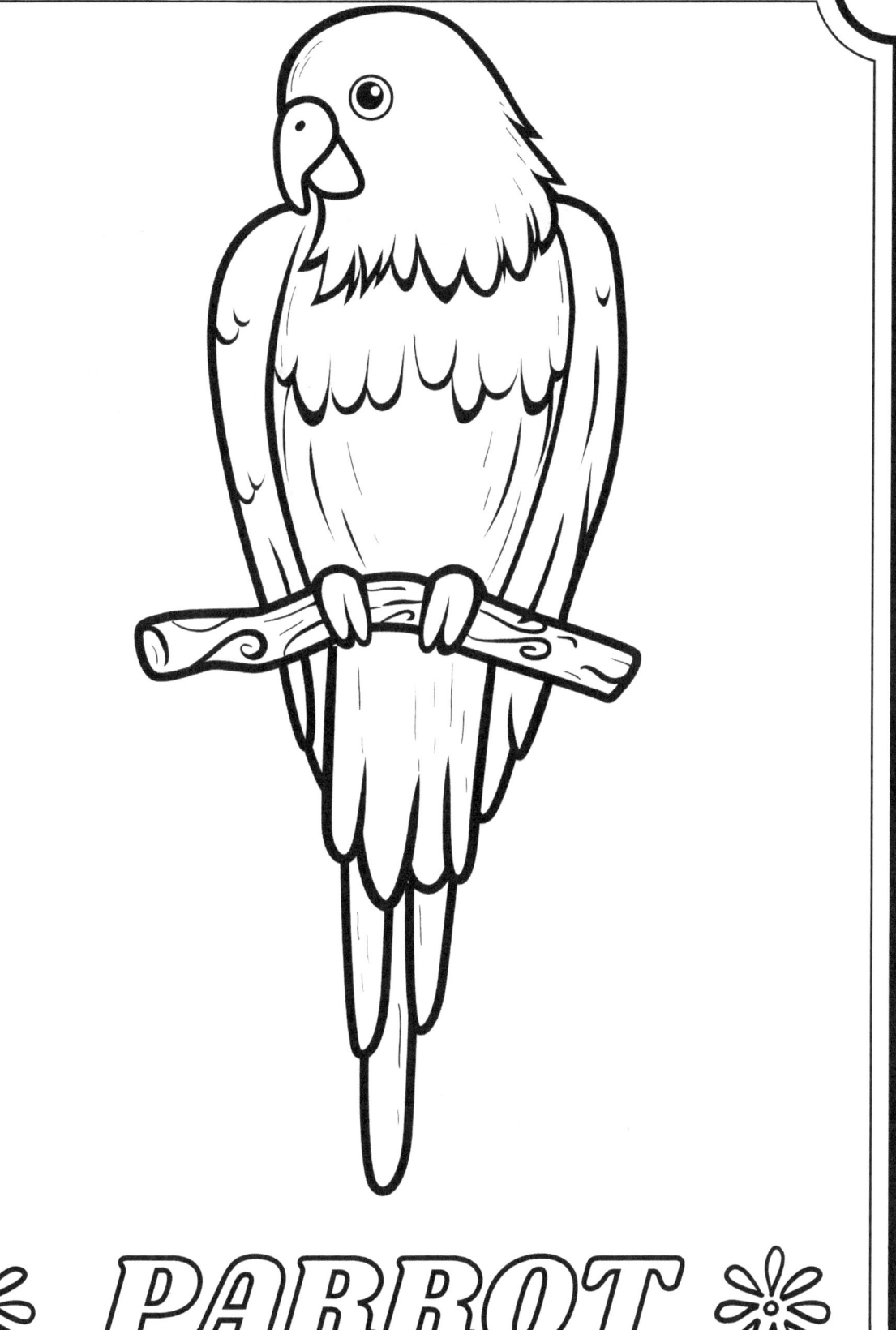

PARROT

17

SEVENTEEN

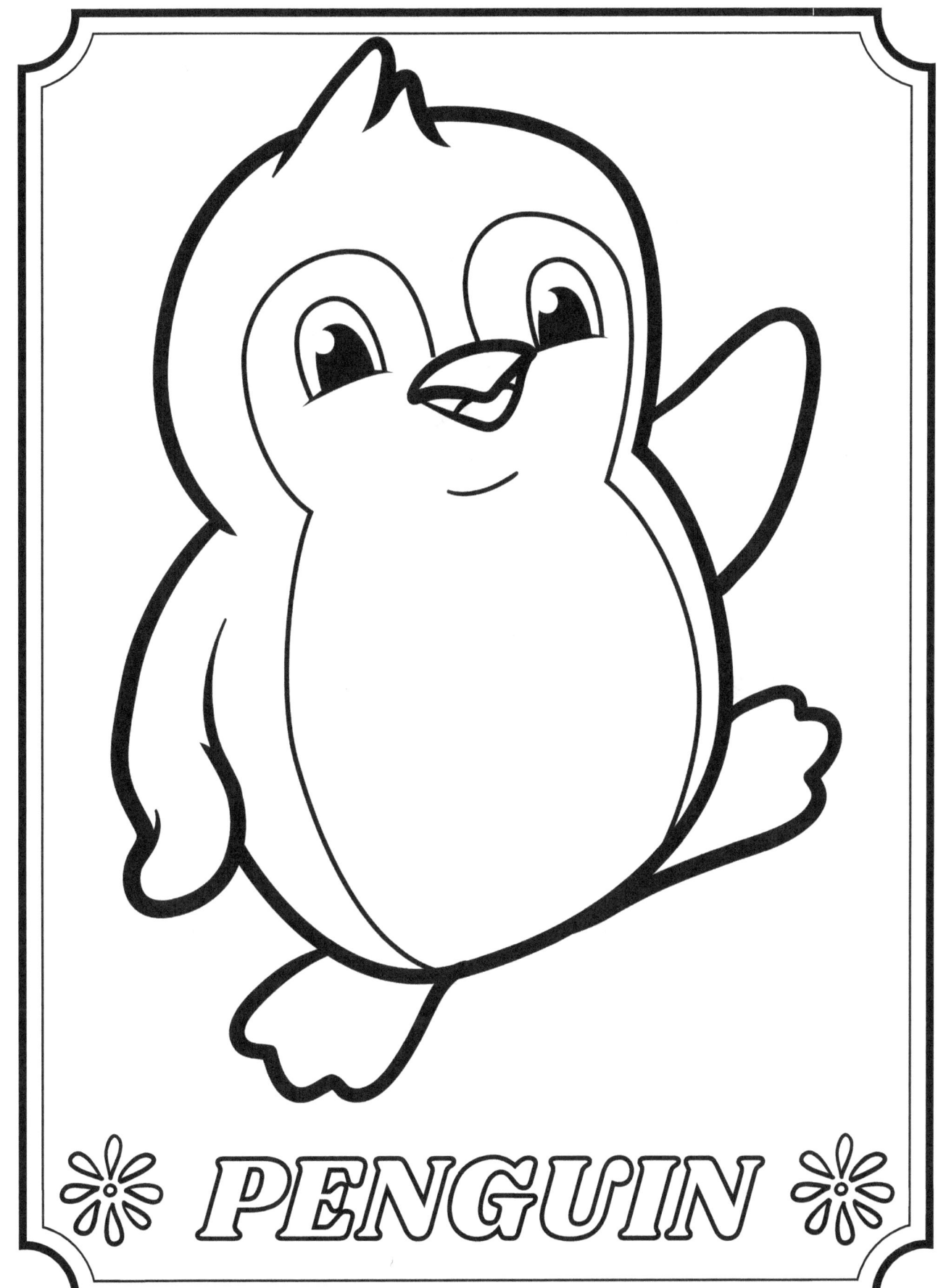

18

EIGHTEEN

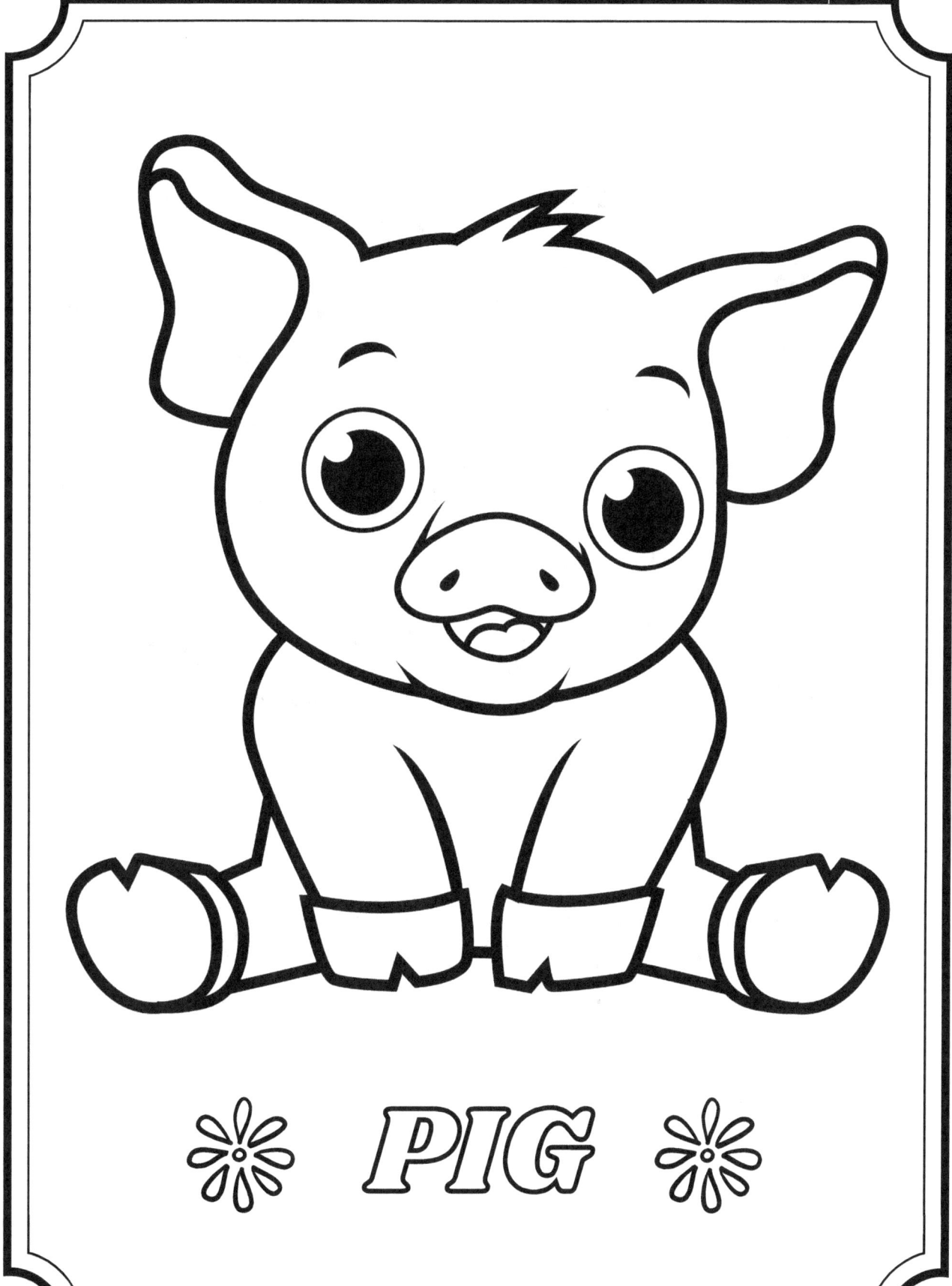

19

NINETEEN

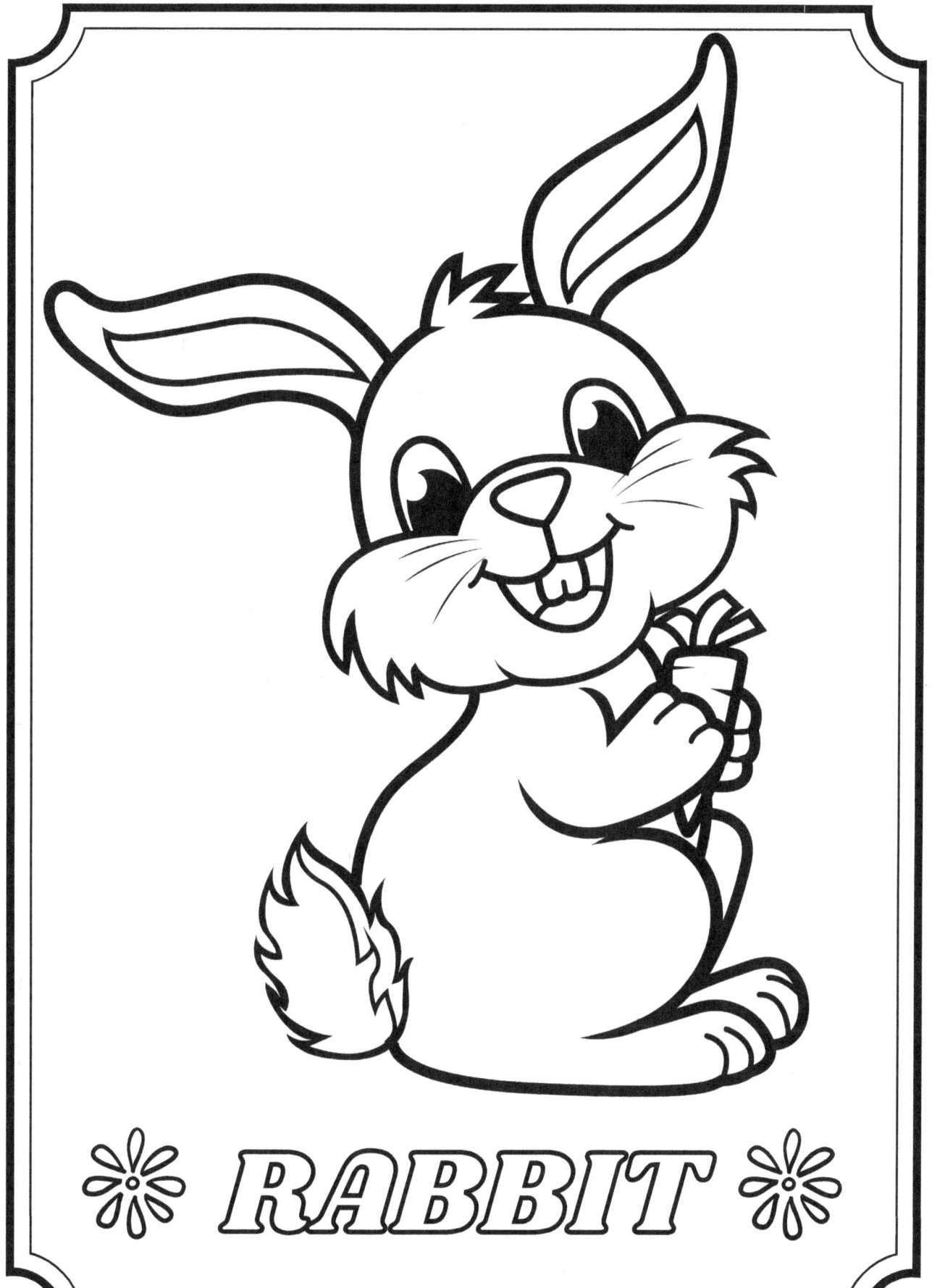

20
TWENTY

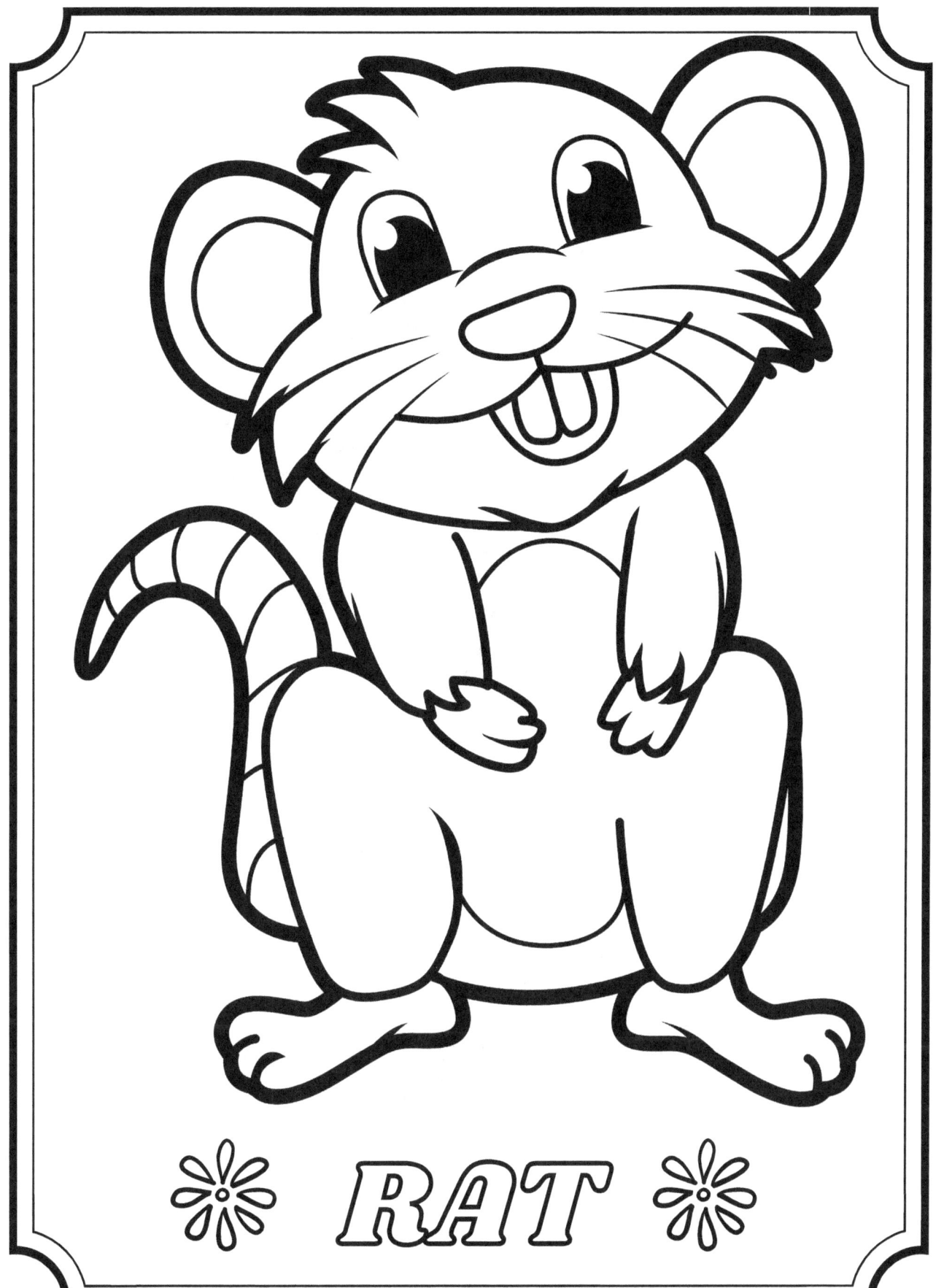

FLOWER

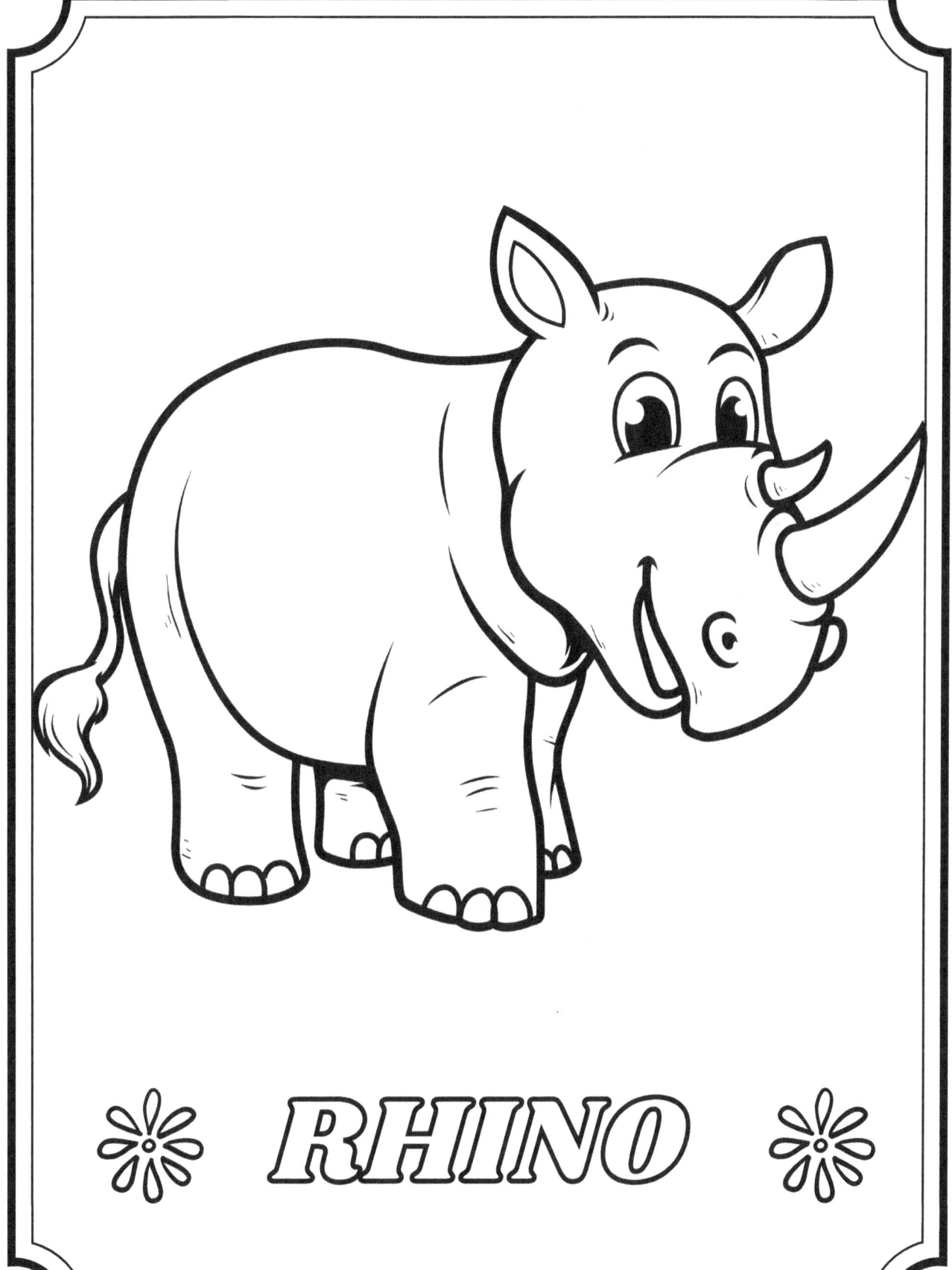

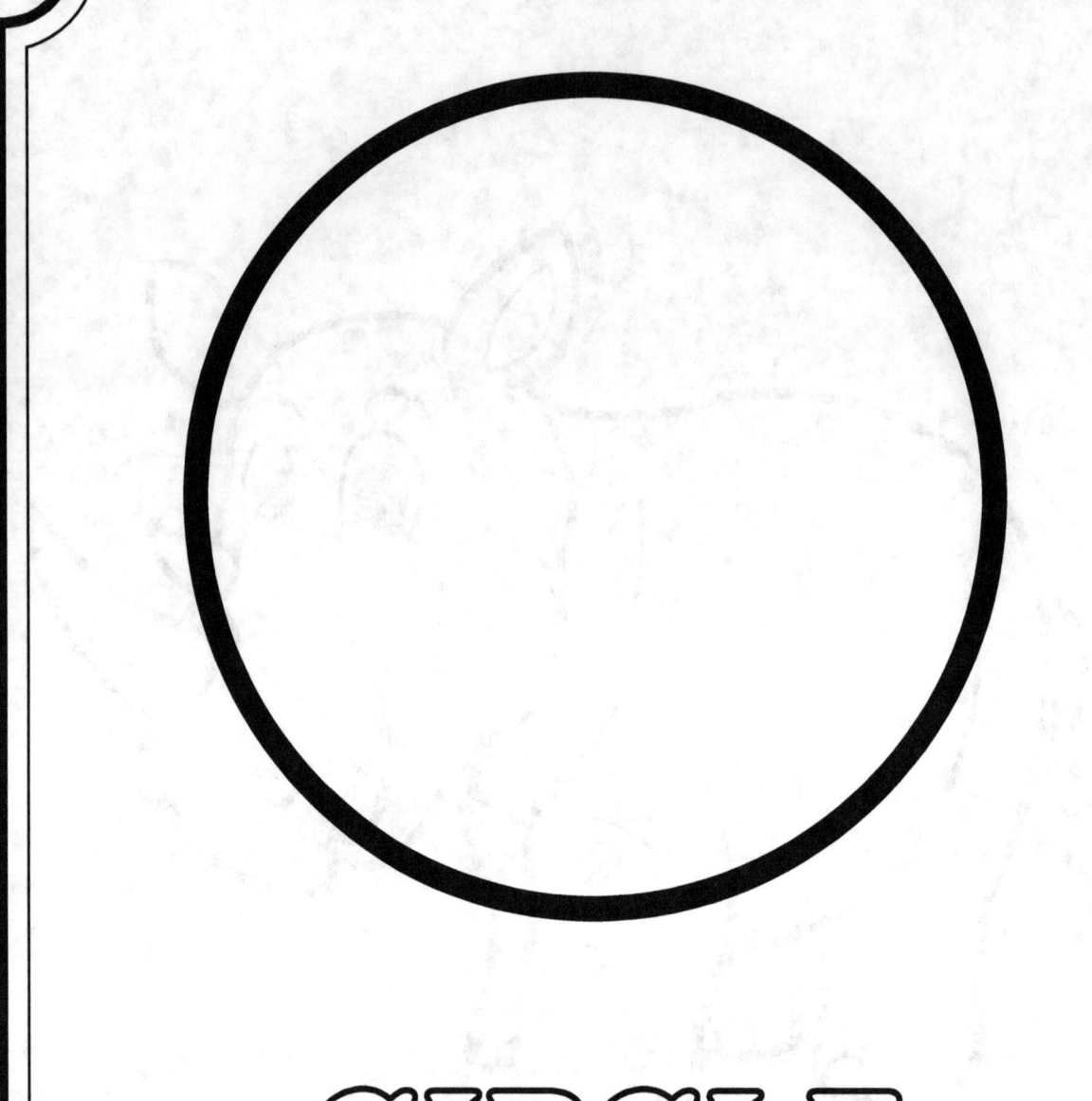

CIRCLE

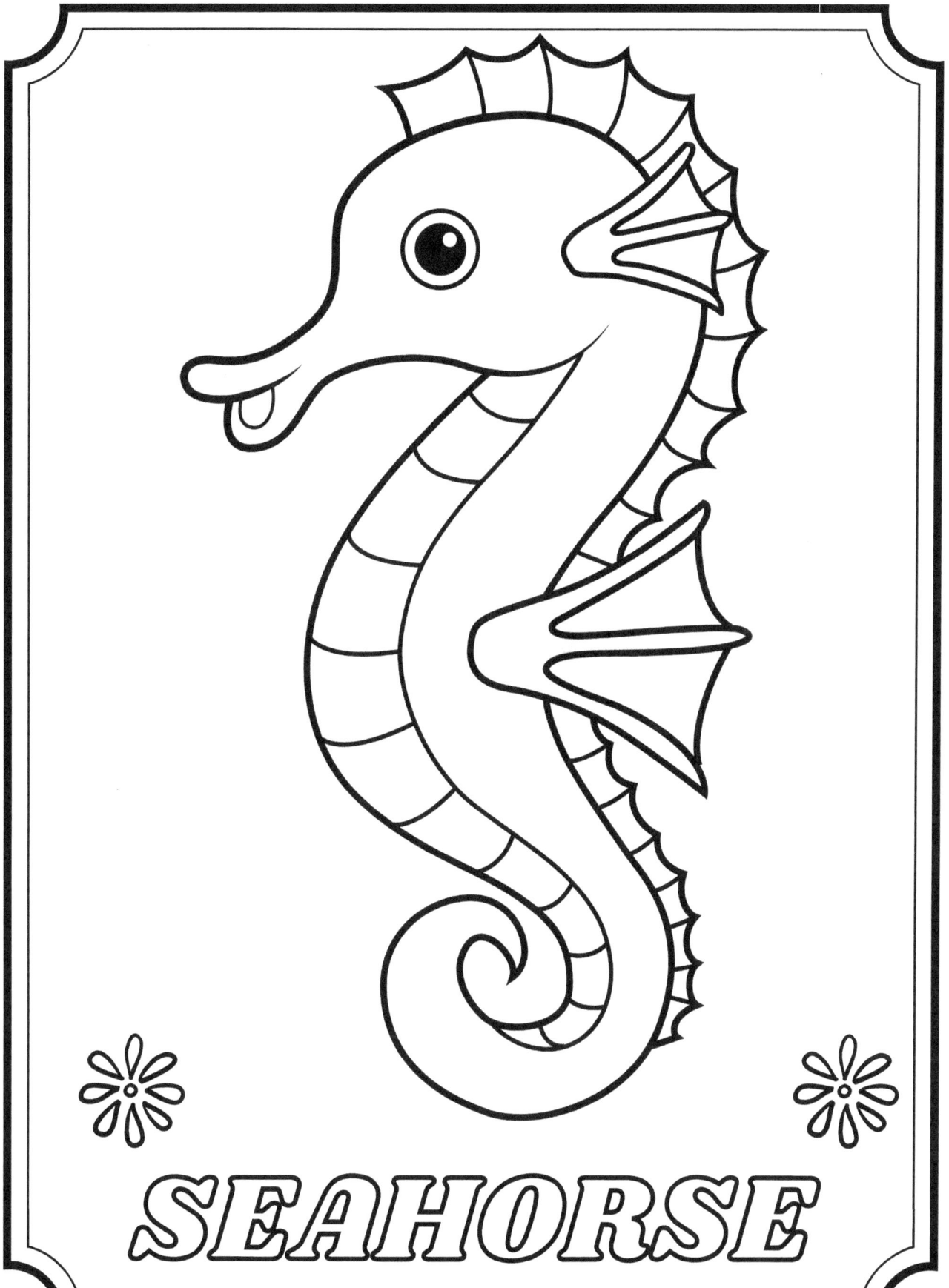

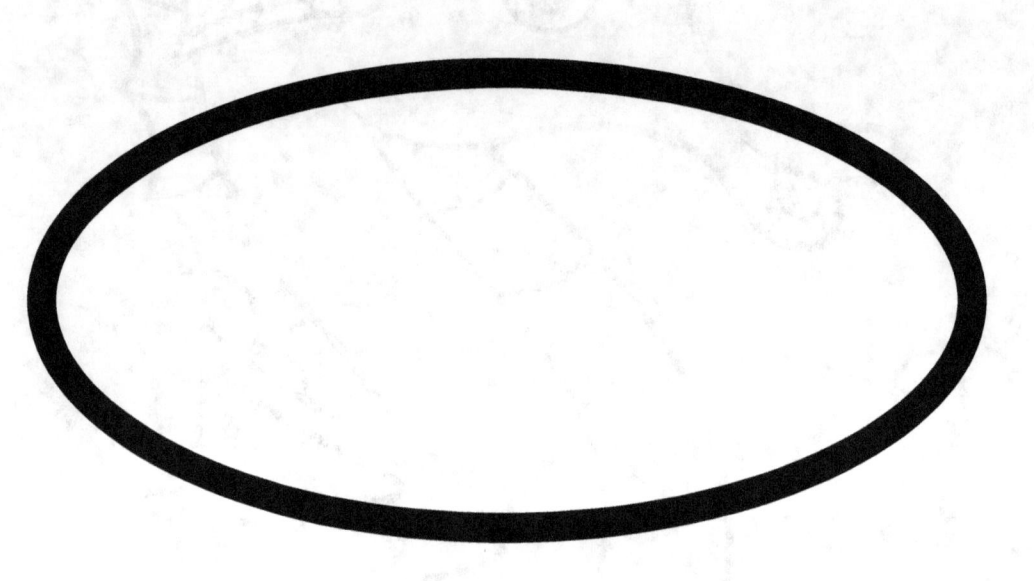

OVAL

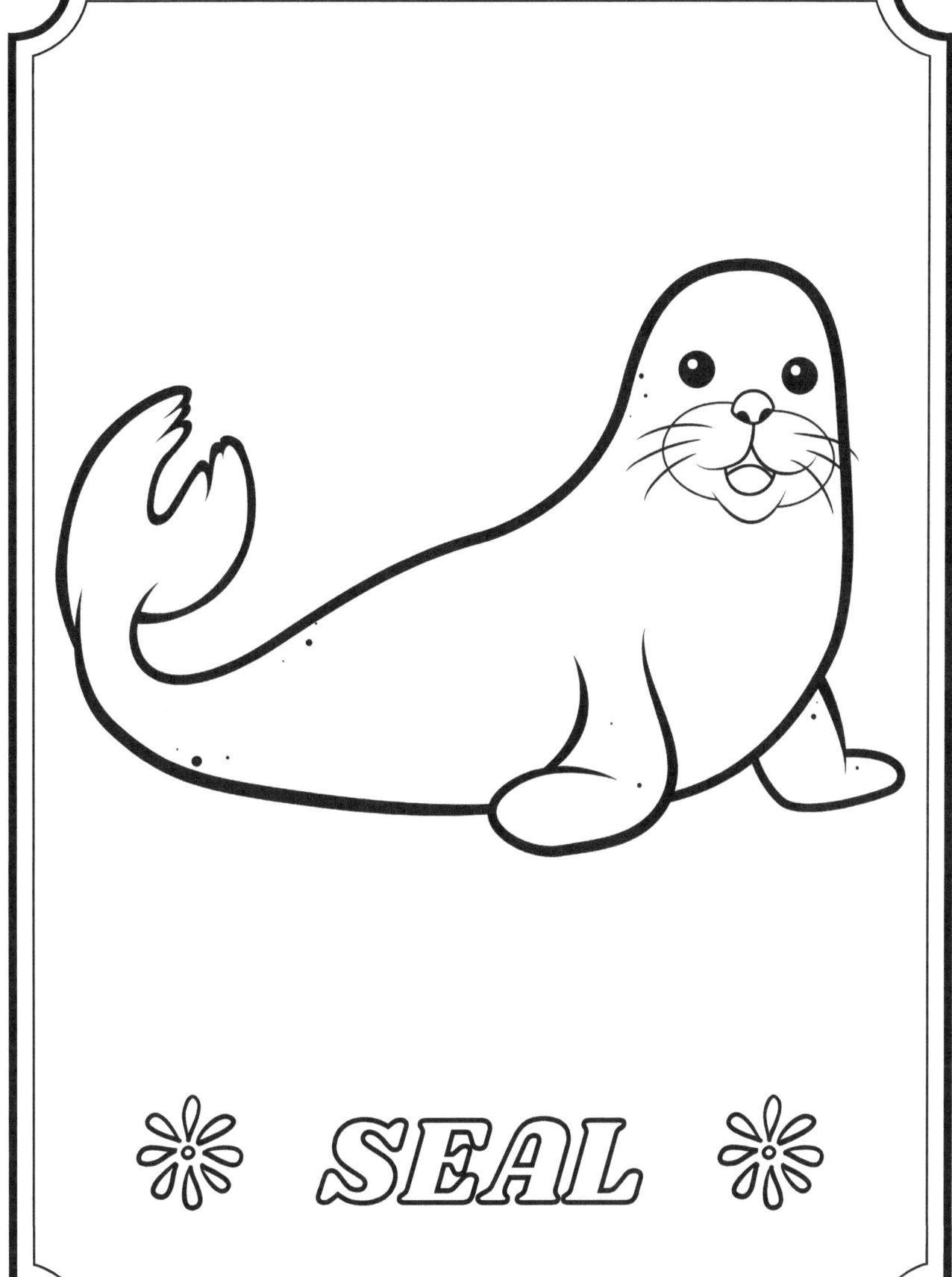

SQUARE

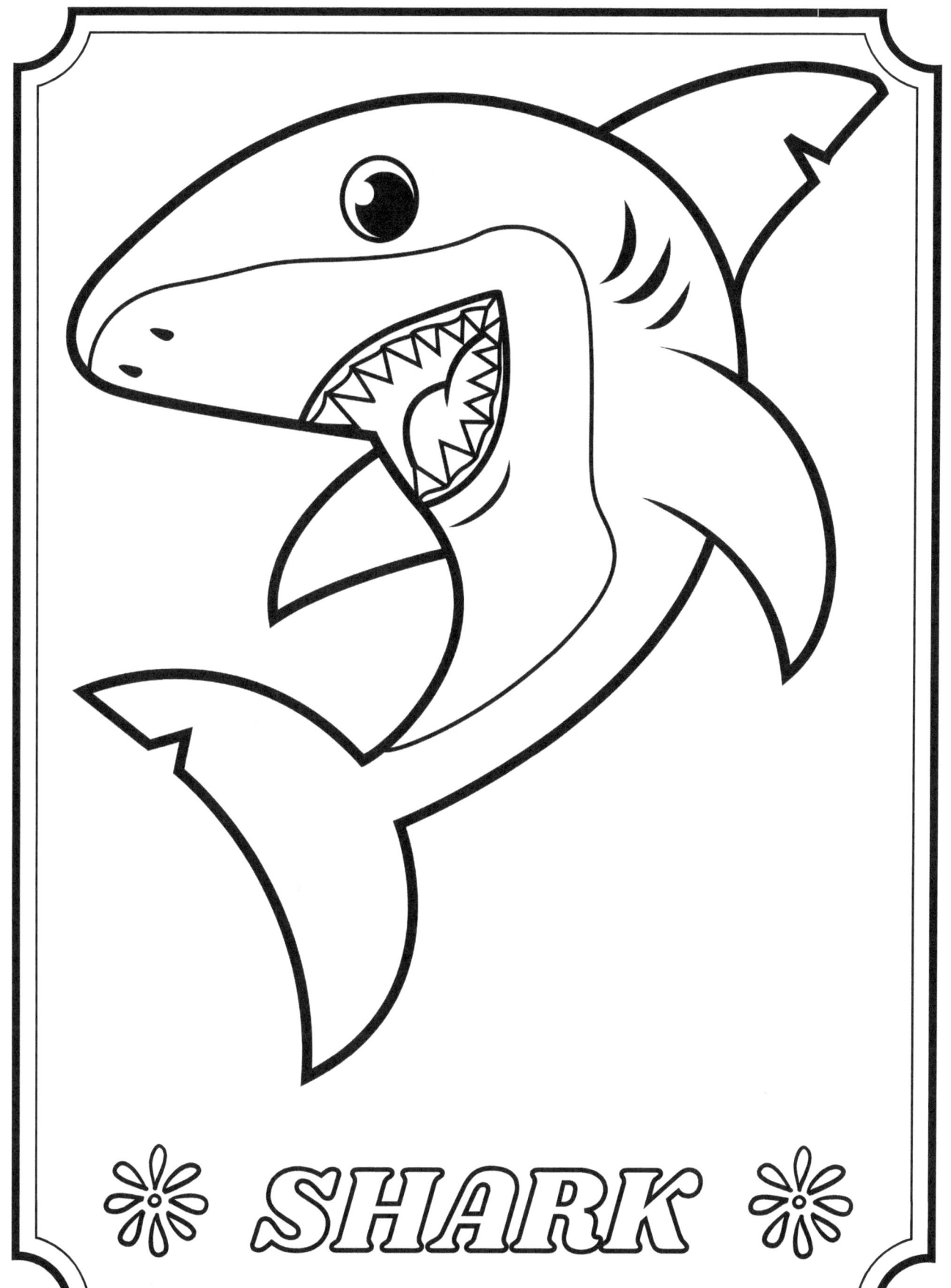

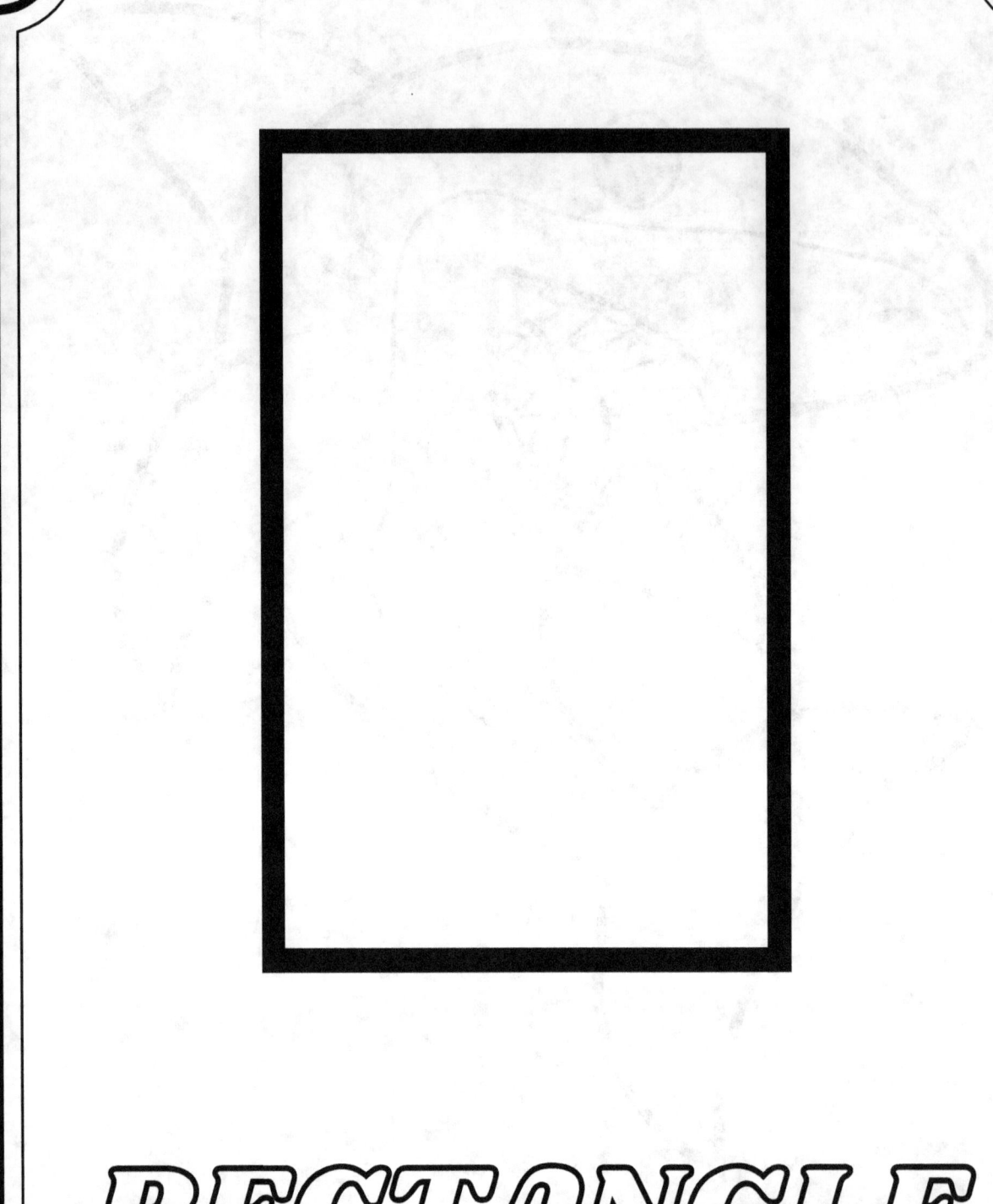

RECTANGLE

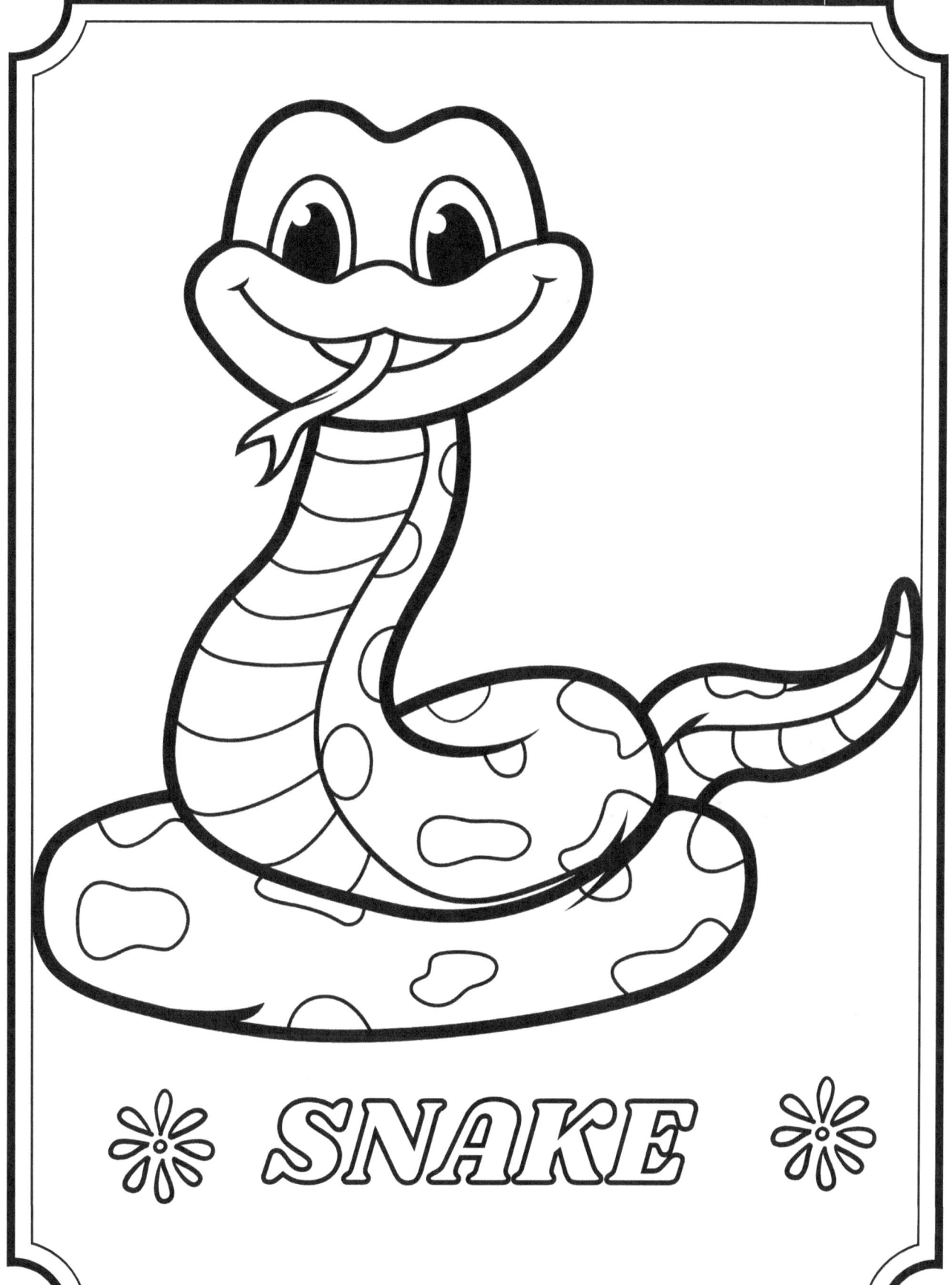

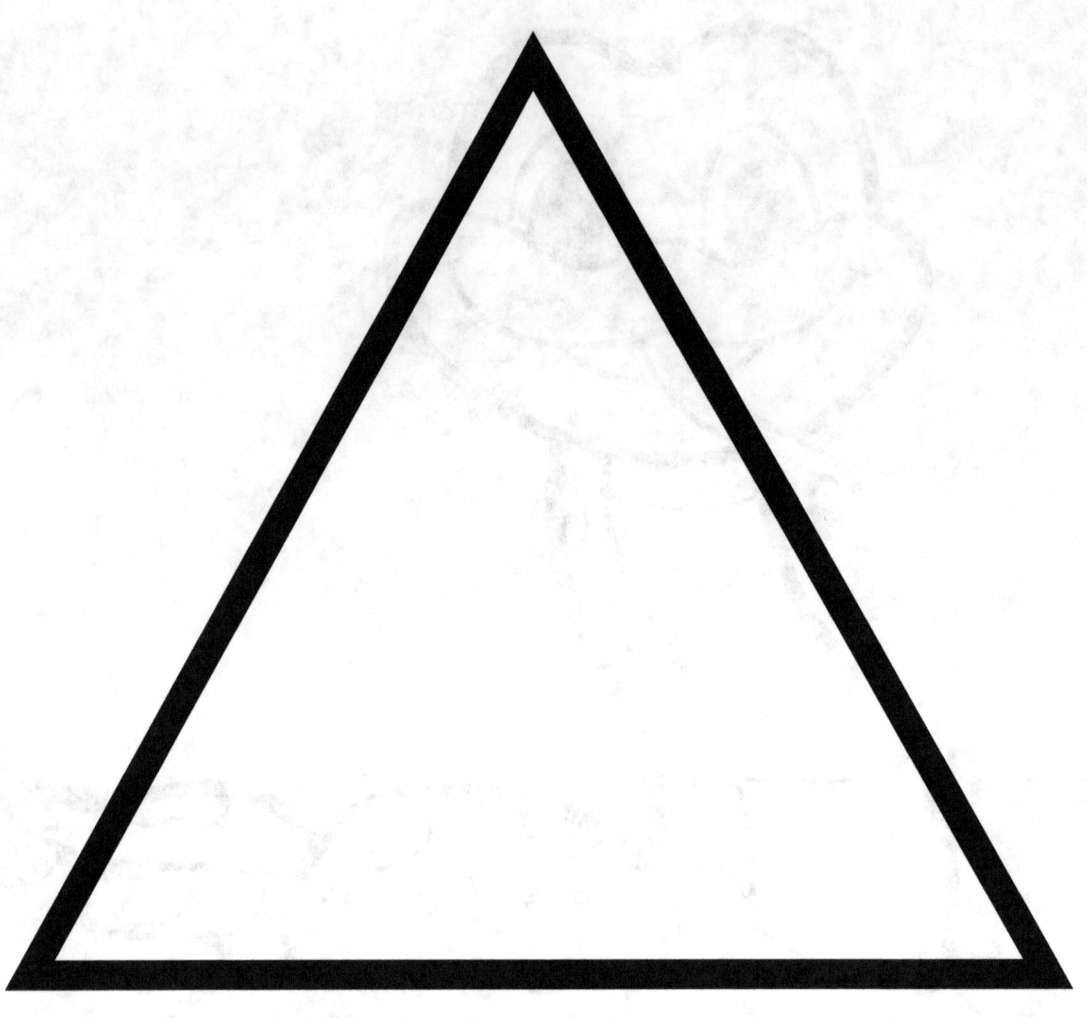

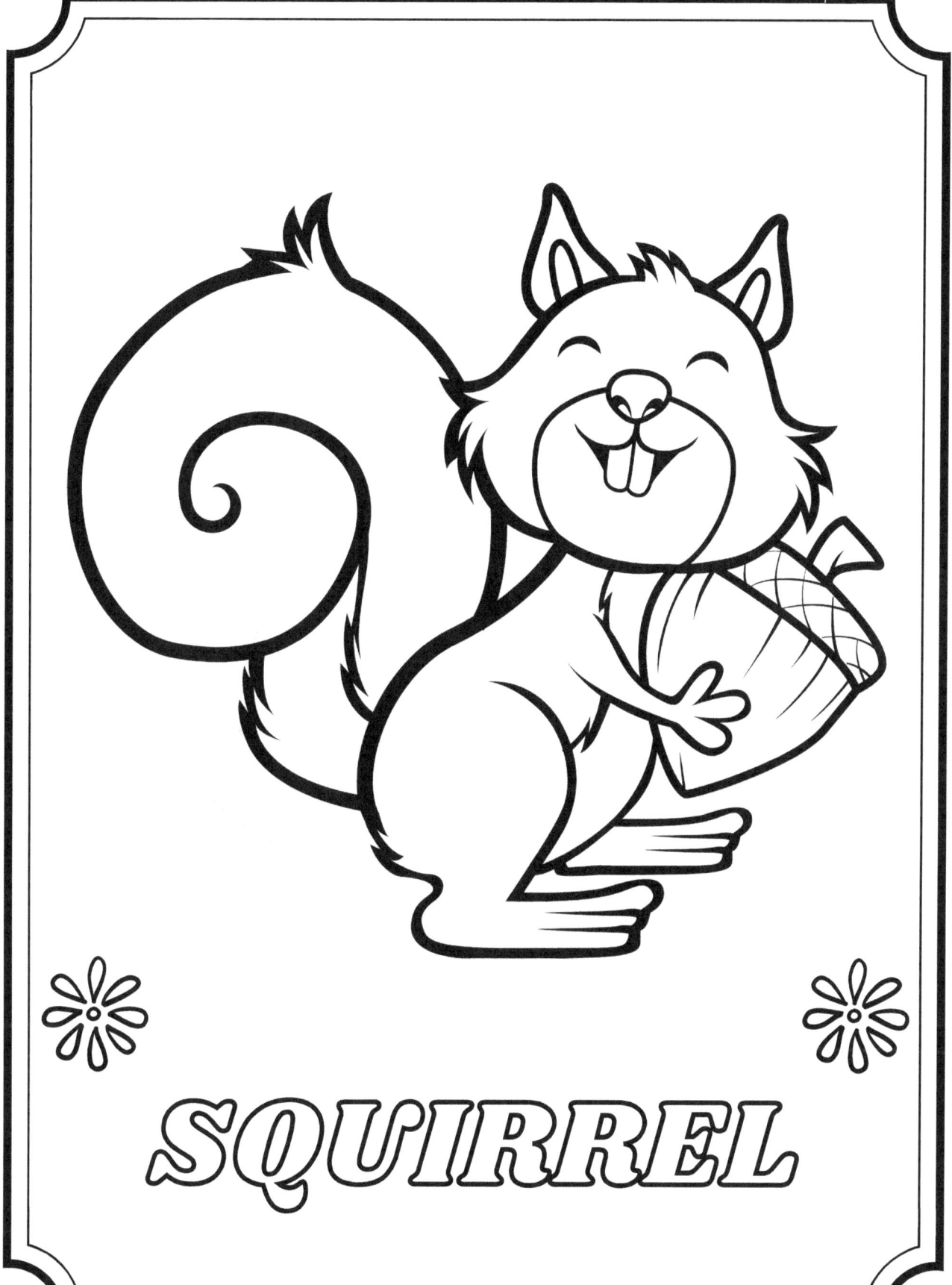

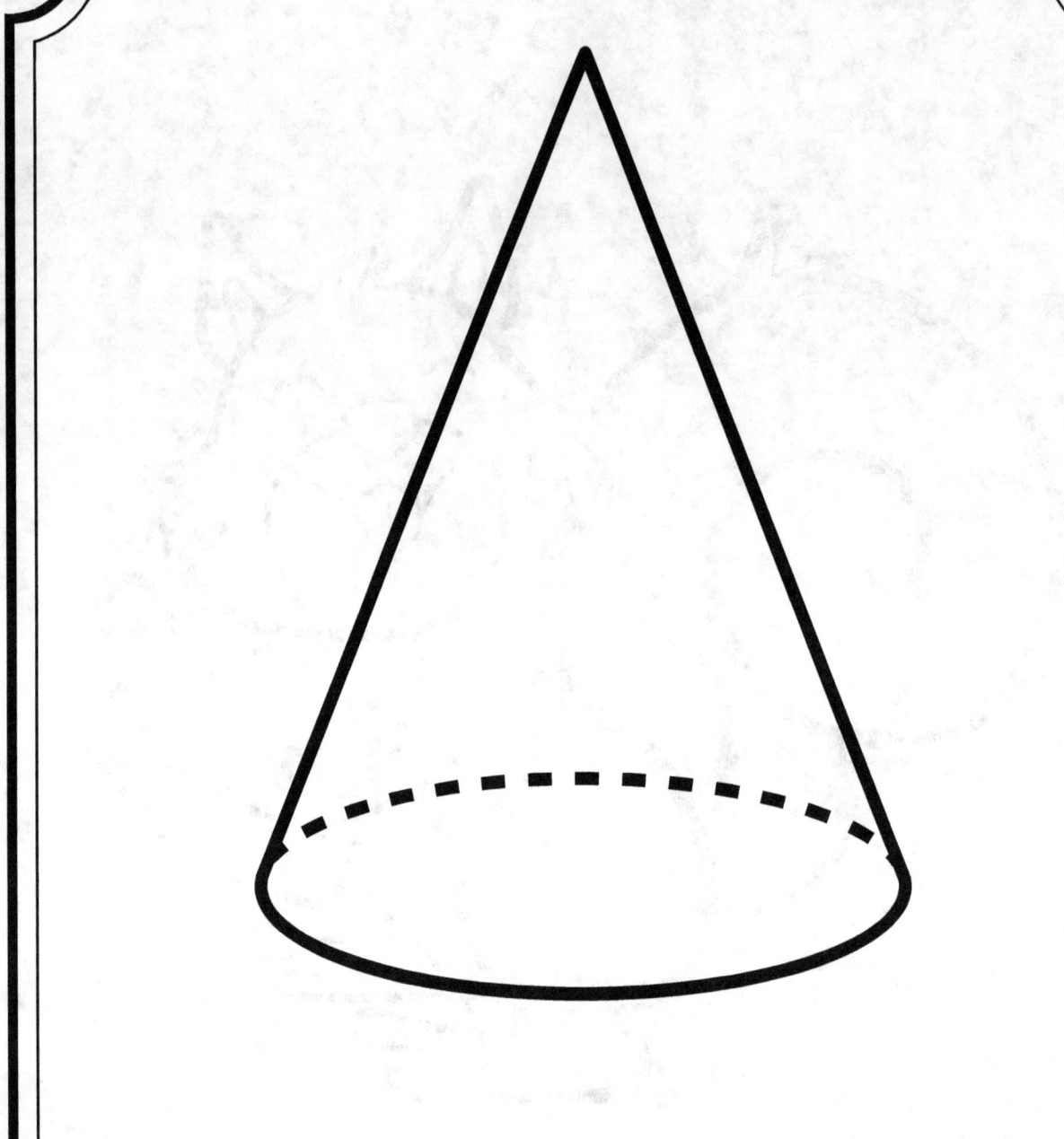

CONE

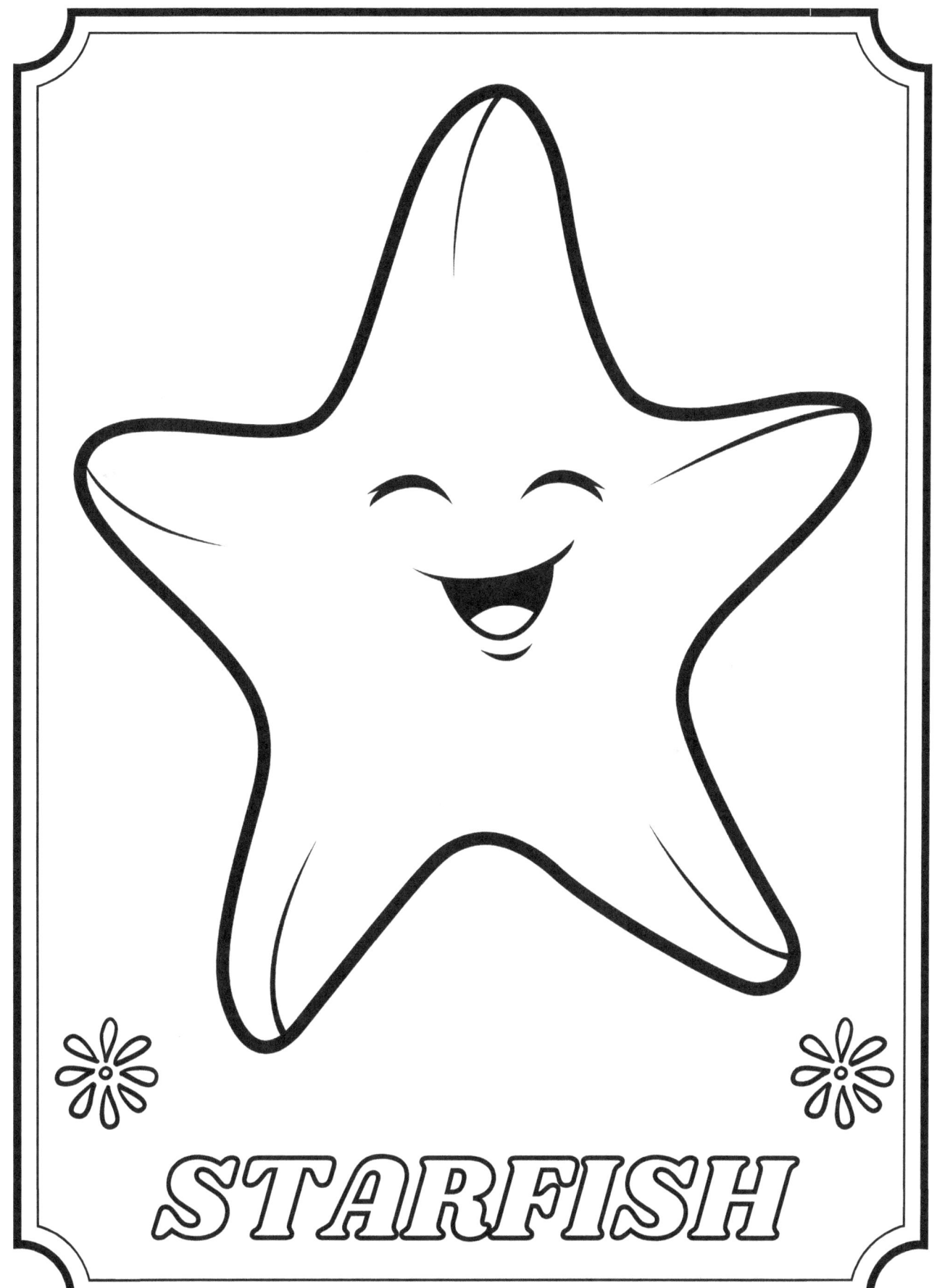

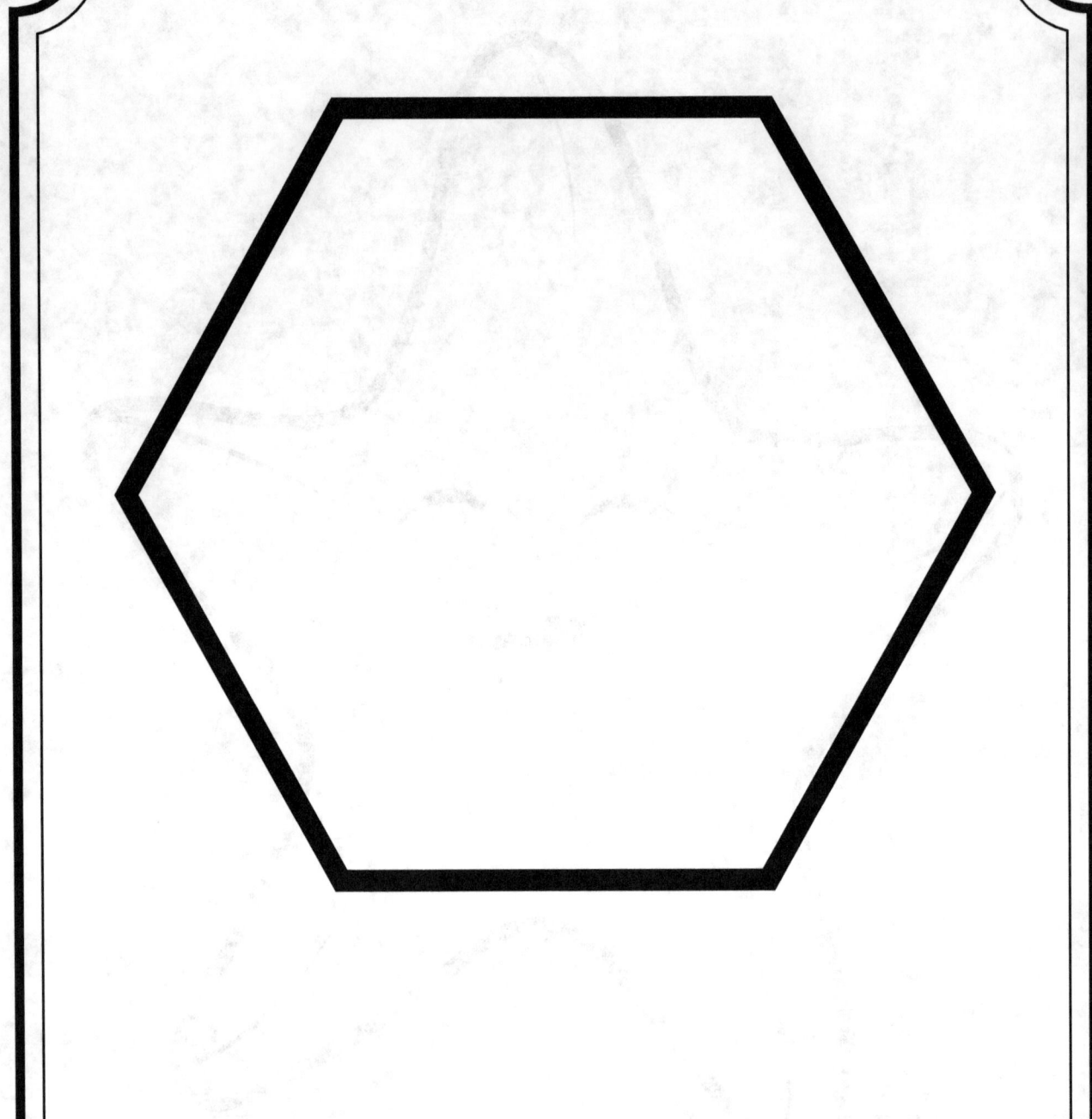

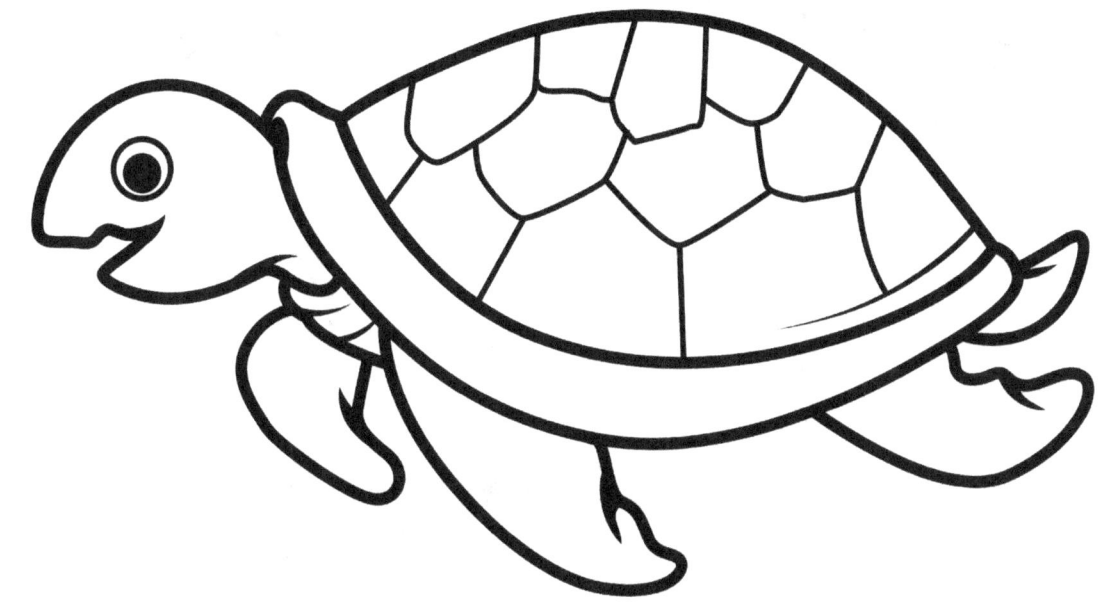

TURTLE

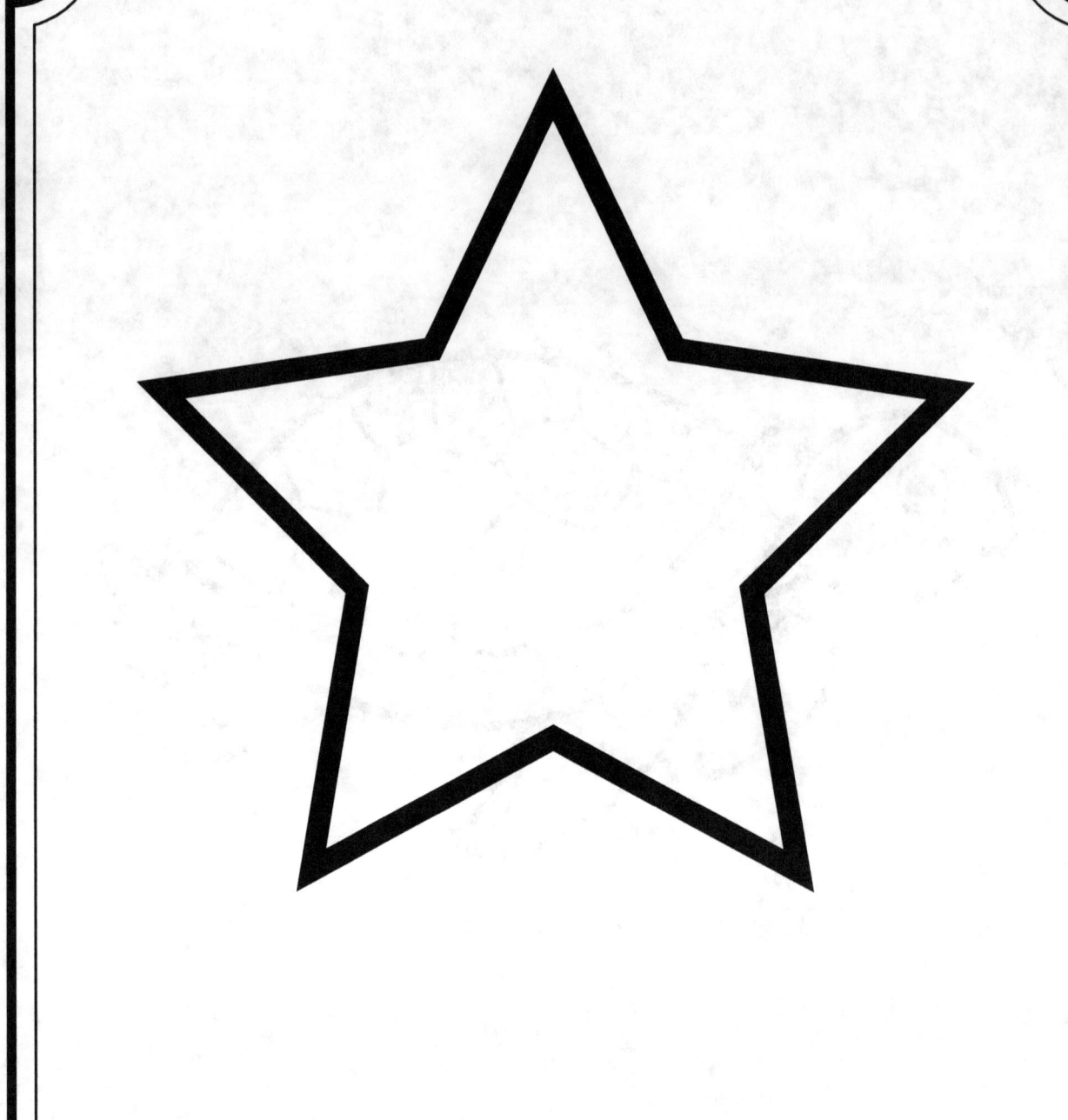

STAR

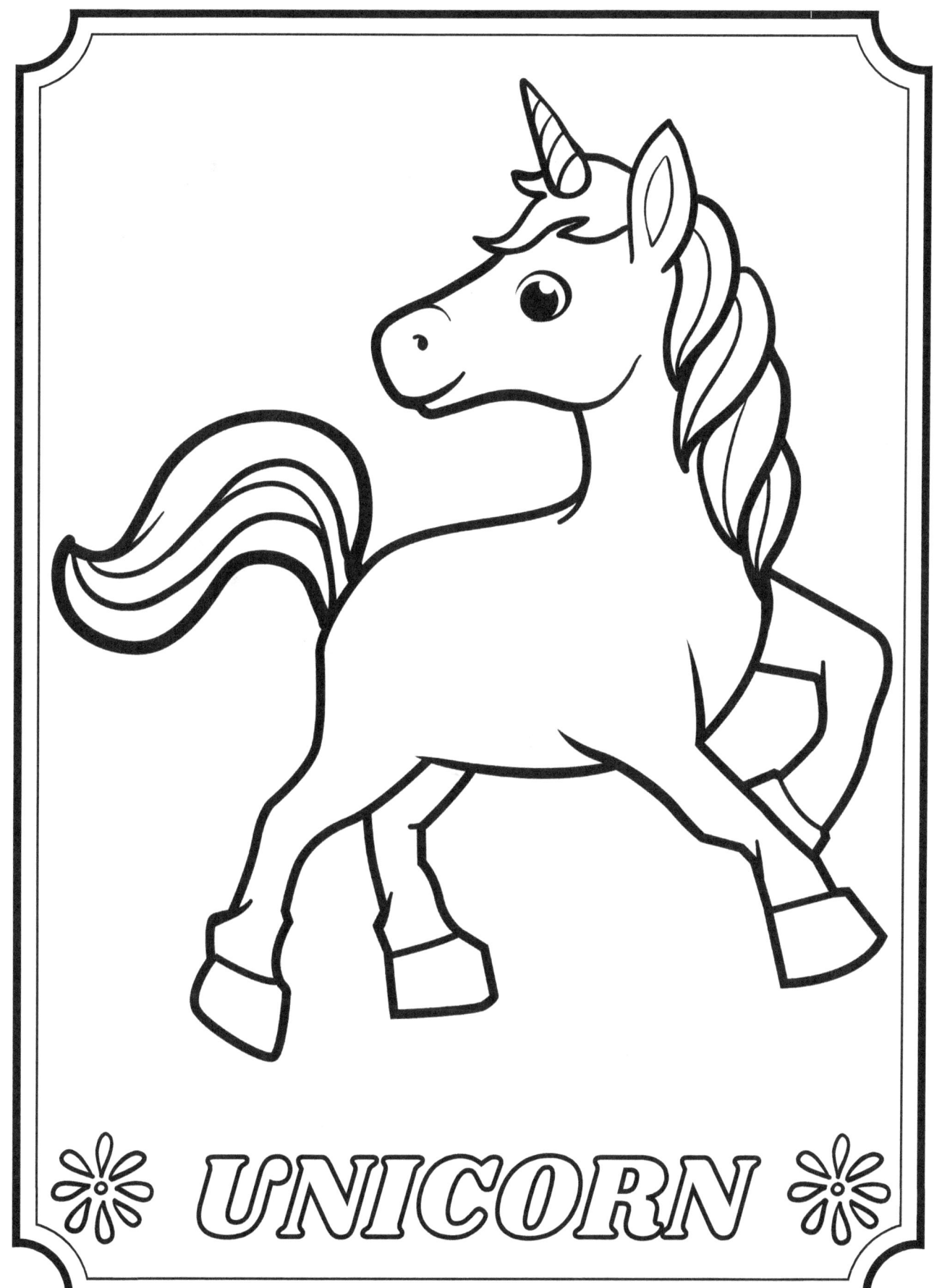

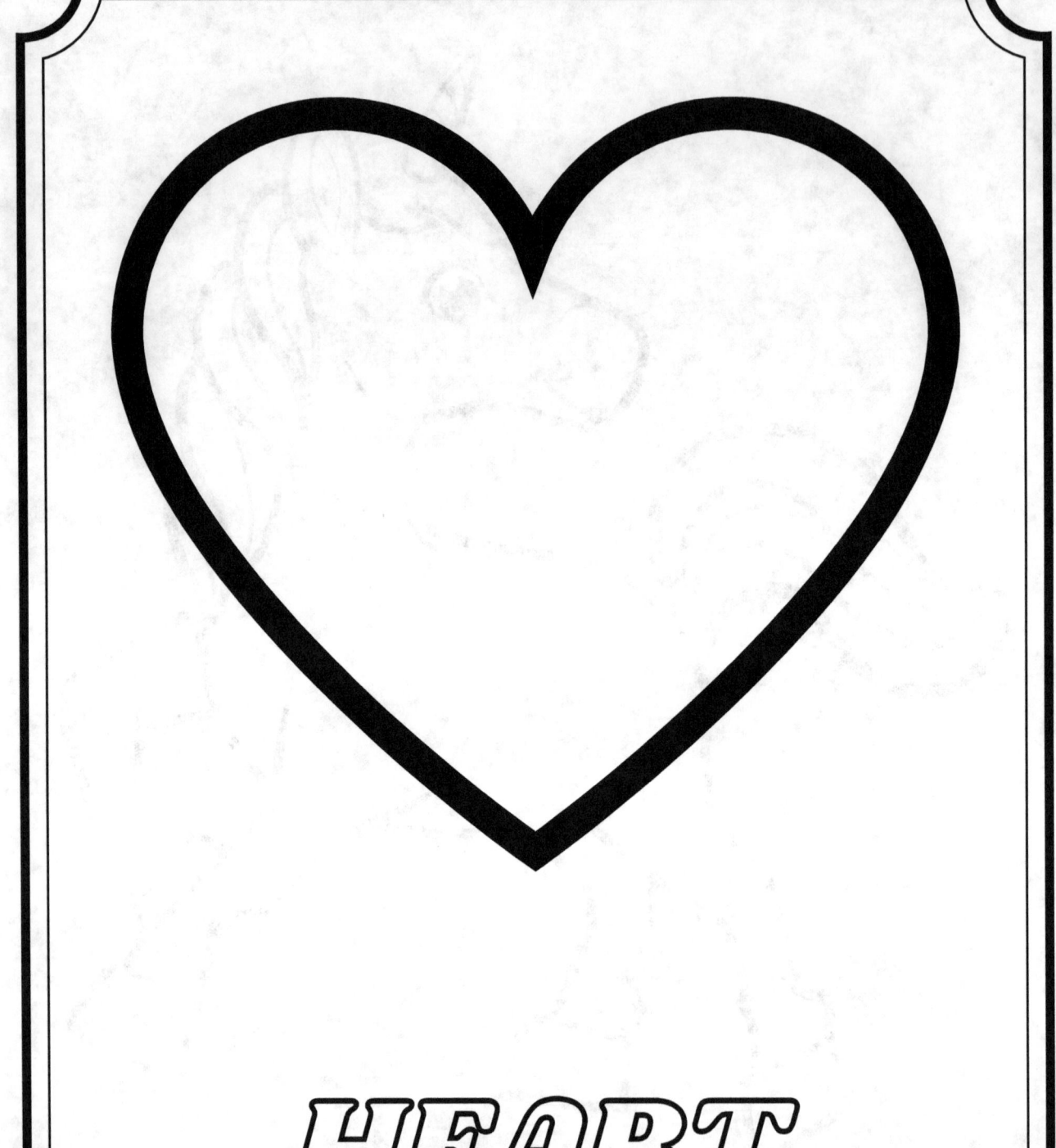

www.ingramcontent.com/pod-product-compliance
Lightning Source LLC
Chambersburg PA
CBHW081500220526
45466CB00008B/2720